Cambridge Elements ≡

Elements in Earth System Governance
edited by
Frank Biermann
Utrecht University
Aarti Gupta
Wageningen University

ENVIRONMENTAL RECOURSE AT THE MULTILATERAL DEVELOPMENT BANKS

Susan Park
University of Sydney

CAMBRIDGE
UNIVERSITY PRESS

CAMBRIDGE
UNIVERSITY PRESS

University Printing House, Cambridge CB2 8BS, United Kingdom

One Liberty Plaza, 20th Floor, New York, NY 10006, USA

477 Williamstown Road, Port Melbourne, VIC 3207, Australia

314–321, 3rd Floor, Plot 3, Splendor Forum, Jasola District Centre, New Delhi – 110025, India

79 Anson Road, #06–04/06, Singapore 079906

Cambridge University Press is part of the University of Cambridge.

It furthers the University's mission by disseminating knowledge in the pursuit of education, learning, and research at the highest international levels of excellence.

www.cambridge.org
Information on this title: www.cambridge.org/9781108702348
DOI: 10.1017/9781108776646

© Susan Park 2020

First published 2020

A catalogue record for this publication is available from the British Library.

ISBN 978-1-108-70234-8 Paperback
ISSN 2631-7818 (online)
ISSN 2631-780x (print)

Environmental Recourse at the Multilateral Development Banks

Elements in Earth System Governance

DOI: 10.1017/9781108776646
First published online: November 2020

Susan Park
University of Sydney

Author for correspondence: Susan Park, susan.park@sydney.edu.au

Abstract: Global governance now provides people with recourse for harm through international grievance mechanisms, such as the independent accountability mechanisms of the multilateral development banks. Yet little is known about how such mechanisms work. This Element examines how IGMs provide recourse for infringements of three procedural environmental rights: access to information, access to participation, and access to justice in environmental matters, as well as environmental protections drawn from the United Nations Guiding Principles and the World Bank's protection standards. A content analysis of 394 original IAM claims details how people invoke these rights. The Sections then unpack how the IAMs provide community engagement through 'problem-solving' and 'compliance investigations' that identify whether the harm resulted from the MDBs. Using a database of all known submissions to the IAMs (1,052 claims from 1994 to mid-2019), the Sections demonstrate how the IAMs enable people to air their grievances, without necessarily solving their problems.

Keywords: international organisations, accountability, environment, human rights, multilateral development banks

ISBNs: 9781108702348 (PB), 9781108776646 (OC)
ISSNs: 2631-7818 (online), 2631-780x (print)

Contents

1 International Recourse for Environmental and Social Harm

Can environmental and social harm, such as species extinction and loss of land, be effectively addressed at the international level? Although harms such as these may be inflicted on individuals, communities, and ecosystems within the confines of territorial borders, rapid changes in the international political economy over the last few decades has increased the possibility of environmental and social harm caused or facilitated by transnational or international actors such as multinational corporations (MNCs) and intergovernmental organisations (Mason 2005). While environmental and social harm caused by actors operating beyond the state is by no means new, over time the volume of interactions has increased, resulting in further environmental degradation with the likelihood for conflict and greater harm (Carmen and Agyeman 2011; Temper et al. 2018). Moreover, corporations, states, and international organisations increasingly work together in public–private partnerships that raise questions as to their responsibility and accountability (Andonova 2017; Biermann 2014).

In response to these trends there has been an attendant proliferation of global governance, such as multilateral environmental agreements (MEAs) and their secretariats that seek to regulate states environmental impact (Biermann and Siebenhuner 2009; Mitchell 2002–2019). Yet states have also allowed transnational private bodies and international organisations the authority to establish global norms and rules (Block-Lieb and Halliday 2017; Park and Kramarz 2019). This authority has extended to the settlement of international disputes, particularly for commercial actors such as foreign investors, with environmental and social implications (Mattli and Dietz 2014; Tienhaara 2009). It has also led to new avenues for people and communities to hold actors to account for environmental and social harm beyond the state (Hertogh and Kirkham 2018).

This section outlines the difference between legal and non-legal avenues for international recourse to highlight an underexamined global trend towards the proliferation of international grievance mechanisms (IGMs), defined as international mechanisms created by transnational or international actors that give affected or potentially affected people the right to seek recourse for the impacts of their activities, especially where they have no access to a liability mechanism.[1] This is important, given arguments that global governance is undemocratic, state driven, and selective in opening up participation (Moravcsik 2004; Tallberg et al. 2013). As grievance mechanisms move to the international level, there needs to be a thorough investigation of how they address environmental and social harm.

---

[1] On the absence of liability mechanisms, see Richards (n.d).

This Element therefore has three aims: first, it identifies the normative standards underpinning international grievance mechanisms globally. It highlights how they seek to uphold procedural environmental rights: specifically, the right to participation, the right to access information, and the right to access justice in environmental matters. To this I add an analysis of how the rights of nature fare in these people-centred recourse processes, given the acceleration of global environmental change and the demands communities make for environmental protection (Park 2019). Investigating the rights of nature is imperative because the environment cannot act for itself and to date has few rights accorded to it (on legal rights accorded to nature, see Kauffman and Sheehan 2019). This is even more compelling considering the global scale and accelerating rate of environmental change (ESG 2018), with precipitous alterations in natural systems (Steffen et al., 2015). The Element is focused on site-specific environmental and social harm, although these do feed into and are affected by larger ecological systems change. Second, the Element examines a class of international grievance mechanisms, the independent accountability mechanisms of the multilateral development banks. This is for three reasons: first, they have amassed considerable experience in responding to environmental and social claims from people harmed by international development projects financed by the MDBs over the last two decades (see Park 2019). Second, they are comparable in function and structure, given they all used the World Bank's Inspection Panel as the template from which to tailor their own mechanisms (Park 2017). This Element questions the activities of the international grievance mechanisms of the World Bank and World Bank Group[2]; the Asian (ADB), African (AfDB), and Inter-American Development Banks (IDB); and the European Bank for Reconstruction and Development (EBRD). Third, analysing these mechanisms is important because as large-scale, high-profile public funders they are 'most likely' cases for international grievance mechanisms to actually operate compared with less transparent private sector (Macdonald and Macdonald 2017) or lesser known and less resourced public funders (Zappile 2016).

---

[2] The International Bank for Reconstruction and Development (IBRD) is popularly known as the World Bank, which also manages funding from the International Development Association (IDA). The World Bank Group is composed of the International Finance Corporation (IFC), a private-sector lender and investor; the Multilateral Investment Guarantee Agency (MIGA), a political risk insurer; and the International Centre for Settlement of Investment Disputes (ICSID), an arbitration body. IFC and MIGA have the same member states as the World Bank on their Boards but have different voting weights, and decisions for IFC and MIGA are made separately from the World Bank and from each other (i.e. by IFC and MIGA management under their executive vice presidents). The president of the World Bank is also the president of the World Bank Group. Over the last decade, there has been a push to bring the separate entities closer together under a single World Bank Group banner. Combined, in 2018, they committed, disbursed, and issued risk coverage amounting to over $45 billion (World Bank 2019).

An important contribution to the debate over the value of having international grievance mechanisms at the international level is to examine how communities use them. I undertook a content analysis of 394 publicly available original grievance claims to the independent accountability mechanisms submitted between 1994 and the end of 2018 by people adversely affected by MDB projects. The analysis reveals that people do seek recourse for the Banks' failure to provide access to participation and access to justice, and they do use the mechanisms as a means for access to justice in environmental matters. It also reveals that people also seek recourse for nature beyond their own dependence on it. Finally, the Element empirically investigates the activities of these IAMs aims. In doing so, it evaluates the procedures established by the mechanisms to provide access to justice in environmental matters through two avenues: 'problem-solving', which entails direct discussion and engagement with communities, the project sponsor, and the Bank to rectify the problem and stop the harm; and 'compliance investigations', which determine whether it was Bank non-compliance with its environmental and social policies that led to the harm. In reviewing a database of all of the claims made publicly available by the IAMs (1,052 cases between 1994 and mid-2019) also highlights how access to justice in environmental matters through the problem-solving process does not necessarily solve people's grievances, given the voluntary nature of engagement with communities for the Banks and (often private sector) project sponsors. While the compliance investigation process does generally hold the Banks to account for contributing to harm through environmental and social policy non-compliance, more research is needed as to whether this in turn adequately addresses claimant's grievances. The remainder of this section situates and details the contours of international grievance mechanisms, before outlining the remainder of the Element.[3]

Legal and Non-legal Forms of International Recourse

Two forms of international recourse, legal and non-legal, are available for people who have suffered physical violence, loss of property and livelihoods, and irreparable environmental damage because of the activities of transnational and international actors. Both are important, and the reason for communities choosing one over the other may rest on several factors, as will be discussed. Legal processes like international courts and tribunals have increased in number (Alter 2014). Of these, some, such as the International Court of Justice,

---

[3] Of the 1,052 cases in the IAM database, only 394 of the original claimants' submissions are publicly accessible. This in part stems from the data collection of the mechanisms themselves, but is also based on whether people want their claims to be confidential or not.

adjudicate disputes over natural resources, and others, such as the World Trade Organisation's Dispute Settlement Mechanism increasingly deal with environmental and human health risks (Foster 2011; Peel 2010). These are state-based legal processes, which may or may not be linked to the needs and desires of those directly harmed. Indeed, states are often complicit with transnational and international actors in economic activities, including the extraction of natural resources, and in financing large-scale infrastructure projects such as mines and roadways that facilitate harm. Moreover, because of past imperial resource extraction, developing states have used international law to protect their sovereign right to exploit natural resources (Pahuja 2011). This permanent right over natural resources rests with the nation, not with individuals or local communities. Obligations attendant to this right have also increased over time to include environmental conservation, to 'respect the rights and interests of indigenous peoples, and a duty to use natural wealth and resources in a sustainable way' (Schrijver 2010: 7–8).

The idea that individuals and communities have rights to their environment appeared in the 1972 Stockholm Declaration (Principle 1), 1992 Rio Declaration (Principle 10), Agenda 21, and in the 1987 World Commission on Environment and Development report (also known as the Bruntland report). Rio specifically 'formulated the link between human rights and environmental protection in … procedural terms' including participation, access to information, and access to redress and remedy. Such procedural rights are beginning to be incorporated into multilateral environmental agreements (Ognibene and Kariuki 2019: 176–7). However, procedural environmental rights are rarely codified on their own in international environmental law (Conca 2015: 74–5). Two exceptions to this are regional United Nations (UN) conventions: the 1998 Convention on Access to Information, Public Participation in Decision-Making and Access to Justice in Environmental Matters, which is housed under the United Nations Economic Commission for Europe (otherwise known as the Aarhus Convention, Mason 2005); and the 2018 Escazú Agreement, a binding regional treaty for Latin America by the United Nations Economic Commission for Latin America and the Caribbean.

Currently, there are forty-seven parties to the Aarhus Convention, with states agreeing to provide their publics with these rights, while the Escazú Agreement has seventeen signatories and one ratification. While not yet a treaty, there is also the 2007 UN Declaration on the Rights of Indigenous Peoples (UNDRIP). The declaration details that states should consult with Indigenous Peoples in managing resources, including that no forcible relocation can occur without their free, prior and informed consent; that Indigenous Peoples have rights to their traditional lands; and that they have the right to redress and to just, fair, and equitable treatment if their land has been taken without free, prior and informed Consent (Schrijver 2010: 72). Multilateral environmental agreements, the regional conventions, and the Declaration relate to how states should advance procedural environmental rights for their citizens. In 2018, the UN Special Rapporteur on Human Rights and the Environment reinforced the need for states to protect these rights (UN 2018).[4]

Recognisably, the main avenue for recourse and remedy for people adversely affected by the activities of transnational and international actors is through national legal or political means. However, there are strong reasons why people may choose international procedures for recourse (Lukas et al. 2016: 4), not least because they may put themselves in grave harm for speaking out to protect their environment (Butt et al. 2019). For this reason, the Escazú Agreement specifically includes protections for environmental defenders (Article 9). Local actors may choose to work with international NGOs to instigate the boomerang process to request international actors to force domestic change (Keck and Sikkink 1998; Matejova et al. 2018). International attention may also provide some protection against state reprisal. Other considerations may also play a deciding role, including the extent to which the transnational or international actor is the primary producer, investor, or financier of the activity contributing to harm, and therefore the best means to stop it (Park 2013). The capacity of the state to address complainants' concerns may also shape the decision to choose international fora.

The second form of recourse, and the focus of this Element, is a non-judicial process of using International Grievance Mechanisms (IGMs).[5] These seek to provide direct recourse for people and their environments adversely affected by the actions of transnational and international actors (Macdonald and Miller Dawkins 2015; Richard 2017).[6] Given that there may be a disjuncture between state-based international law and the interests of people and ecosystems, this Element does not examine international law as a form of recourse. Rather it probes how non-judicial processes work to ameliorate environmental and social harm when claims are instigated by people on behalf of their communities and ecosystems. This is especially important as IGMs may ascertain that they can only play a role if judicial recourse cannot or has not been instigated.

---

[4] The United Nations Environment Programme also devised the Bali Guidelines in 2010 for how states should meet Rio Principle 10, closely adhering to the Aarhus Convention (Ognibene and Kariuki 2019: 190; UNEP 2010).

[5] Most non-judicial mechanisms do not claim to offer a remedy that will solve the problem, focusing instead on the provision of recourse or the ability to air grievances that may lead to redress, or a means of amending the situation (through, for example, compensation for loss).

[6] Also known as non-state-based non-judicial grievance mechanisms (NSBGM), Zagelmeyer et al. 2018.

Types of International Grievance Mechanisms

There are a variety of different international grievance mechanisms – from the MDBs' independent accountability mechanisms, to ombudsmen, to multi-stakeholder forums that transnational and international actors may operate globally, regionally, or at the local level. The independent accountability mechanisms of the MDBs seek to provide recourse for people to air their grievance if they identify that the social and environmental harm has been caused by the acts or omission of the Banks (McIntyre and Nanwani 2019). An example of the independent accountability mechanisms is the Inspection Panel of the World Bank (World Bank 2019). A grievance is defined as 'a perceived injustice evoking an individual's or a group's sense of entitlement, which may be based on law, contract, explicit or implicit promises, customary practice, or general notions of fairness of aggrieved communities' (UN 2011: 27). This compares and increasingly overlaps with an ombudsman, which is a body that 'offers independent and objective consideration of complaints, aimed at correcting injustices caused to an individual as a result of maladministration' (International Ombudsman Institute 2012: Preamble). Examples include the European Ombudsman within the European Union (EU), the Compliance Advisor/Ombudsman (CAO) for the World Bank Group, and the Ombudsman for the United Nations (UN), although the latter addresses staff grievances rather than those externally affected by the actions of the UN (Hoffman and Megret 2005).

These two categories overlap: the Compliance Advisor Ombudsman of the World Bank Group and the EU Ombudsman both seek to correct injustices through engagement with aggrieved communities and individuals primarily but may also investigate the cause of the harm in order to stop it.[7] For example, while the CAO prioritises its Ombud's role in order to address grievances, it can also undertake a compliance investigation that identifies whether the World Bank Group was responsible for the harm through lending, investing, or guaranteeing an international development project. Many Ombuds also have 'own-motion' powers that enable them to trigger investigations as the EU and the CAO have (Carl 2018: 18). In comparison, the World Bank Inspection Panel is an independent accountability mechanism that can only investigate the cause of the harm through a compliance investigation triggered by claimants. It cannot

---

[7] Under the Maastricht Treaty, the European Ombudsman has been empowered to respond to citizens and peoples residing in the EU regarding complaints of maladministration of the EU's offices, bodies, agencies, and institutions. It may also instigate its own investigations in the public interest. The European Ombudsman relied on a soft-law European Code of Good Administrative Behaviour as the basis for its work; this was later incorporated as Article 41, the Right to Good Administration, in the binding 2009 EU Charter of Fundamental Rights (Hofmann 2017: 3–4, 9).

directly mediate with complainants to address harm. Its findings provide indirect recommendations to address the grievance that instantiated the complaint. While all the independent accountability mechanisms for the MDBs were designed similarly, over time they have all taken on both roles, directly seeking to address grievances, with the capacity to investigate cause (Park 2017).[8]

To date, research on the MBDs' independent accountability mechanisms, particularly the World Bank Inspection Panel, has focused on their creation, structure, and impacts in terms of holding the Banks to account for (non) compliance with their environmental and social safeguard policies, procedures, and guidelines (Park 2017). This has implications for international law (Naude Fourie 2016), the accountability and legitimacy of the Banks (Sovacool 2017; Zalcberg 2012), and their development approach (Balaton-Chrimes and Haines 2015). However, it is important to examine how affected people use the different processes in seeking to have environmental and social grievances addressed.

For example, the first claim to the African Development Bank's (AfDB) Independent Accountability Mechanism, in 2007, came from the Ugandan National Association of Professional Environmentalists who sought a compliance investigation into the environmental and social impacts of the Bujagali dam. They wanted to determine whether the large-scale adverse environmental and social impacts of the dam, including climate and water impacts and the potential increasing cost of electricity, were the result of acts or omissions by the AfDB in meeting its own environmental and social policies (IRM 2007). The results of the investigation would then inform any changes the Bank would need oversee in order to ensure the project was environmentally and socially compliant.[9] This compares with a local association in Morocco, the Chichaoua Province Development and Law Association, submitting a claim to the same mechanism in 2010 to address the impacts on twelve farmers and six landowners of building the Marrakech–Agadir Motorway. The impacts of the motorway included, among other things, the construction affecting the stability of houses in the village, separating farmers from their pastures, not providing

---

[8] After more than two years of deliberations, in March 2020 the World Bank approved changes to its Inspection Panel. It now has a Dispute Resolution Service akin to the problem-solving functions of the other IAMs and will begin to operate to address environmental and social harm directly from September 2020. Previously, the Bank had a Dispute Resolution Service in-house for helping member states address grievances; this change makes the process independent of Bank Management and under the Inspection Panel. Because the World Bank's internal Dispute Resolution Service was advisory for member states rather than mandatory and engaged with communities, it is not analysed here.

[9] The dam was also being co-financed by the World Bank and the International Finance Corporation and would also receive claims to investigate those financiers' adherence to their policies and mediate with claimants in the latter's case (Park 2019).

canals necessary for irrigation, and redirecting natural water flows away from farmers while facilitating flooding (IRM 2010). In this case, the Bank's Independent Accountability Mechanism was able to facilitate a successful agreement between the requestors, the Bank, and the company undertaking the project regarding six of the eight issues of concern to claimants (IRM 2011: 12).[10] How affected people use the mechanisms is therefore important for understanding whether environmental and social grievances can be addressed.

The outline for the remainder of the Element is as follows: Section 2 explores the human rights and standards for environmental protection upheld by IGMs, pinpointing how they provide recourse for procedural environmental rights. The two normative standards in use are the Guiding Principles for Business and Human Rights (GPs) in relation to human rights and transnational corporations and other business enterprises established by the UN Special Representative of the Secretary-General John Ruggie, and the standards set by the World Bank that have been emulated by other public and private development funders. IGMs have proliferated rapidly and are now used by a range of actors including the MDBs (Park 2017; Zappile 2016), bilateral agencies (Hunter 2008), and corporations and industries (Zagelmeyer et al. 2018). While the spread of such mechanisms is laudable, there remains a dearth of evidence that these mechanisms are effective in providing recourse. The section outlines the type of criteria available to determine whether IGMs provide effective access to justice in environmental matters, and how this compares with our knowledge of their practices. Finally, the section highlights how the 'citizen-driven accountability process' of the IGMs (Lewis 2012) raises concerns that access to justice in environmental matters through IGMs places an undue burden on people to demonstrate harm, which may not capture the full extent of environmental damage.

Sections 3 and 4 investigate the procedures of the international accountability mechanisms of the MDBs. The MDBs are one of the primary means through which states provide official development assistance (OECD 2018). They provide loans, guarantees, and technical assistance to developing countries for development projects. Despite numerous safeguards, the implementation of infrastructure and extractive and energy projects have significant consequences for local communities and ecosystems. For twenty-five years, the World Bank has had its Inspection Panel to provide recourse for grievances from project-affected communities. Yet physical violence, loss of property and livelihoods, damage to ecosystems, and harmful impacts on Indigenous Peoples continue to occur because of projects financed by the Bank. To date, there is little evidence

---

[10] Requestors and claimants are used interchangeably.

as to whether the claims process actually leads to remedies for people affected by MDB-financed projects; and the work that has been done thus far is case specific (Clark et al. 2003; Fox and Brown 1998; Rodrigues 2003; Ziai 2016). Investigating the standards and procedures of the IAMs locates people and the environment at the forefront of the analysis rather than as a by-product for assessing MDB non/compliance with their own policies.

Section 3 probes whether the IAMs can provide access to justice in environmental matters through problem-solving. Problem-solving entails consultation, mediation, dialogue, conciliation, and dispute resolution to redress the grievance. The section details the content analysis of 394 publicly accessible original grievance claims submitted to the IAMs.[11] It identifies if claimants were seeking recourse for breaches of environmental procedural standards such as access to information and participation. In addition, the content analysis identifies whether claimants were concerned with environmental harms beyond how they affect people (or the rights of nature). After identifying the main grievances people bring to the IAM for problem-solving, the section analyses data accumulated on all the known claims to the IAMs between 1994 and mid-2019 that are publicly available (Park 2019). This is done to ascertain whether people are better off after engaging in problem-solving. Section 4 repeats the content analysis and the review of the outcomes of the cases submitted to the IAMs but this time for compliance investigations in order to determine whether the process of investigating the Banks for environmental and social policy noncompliance provides recourse for procedural environmental rights and the rights of nature. Compliance investigations are undertaken by the IAM and include desk reviews of the project documents, interviews with Bank project officers and management, and project site visits. In this process, claimants are interviewed but do not otherwise play an active role. They may be allowed to comment on the completed investigation report before it goes to the Bank's Board. The Bank's board of directors (member states) cannot change the report's outcomes, but they can determine how the Bank should respond to its findings of (non)compliance with environmental and social policies. This section seeks to know whether people are people are better off after triggering these mechanisms, and which process provides access to justice, and for what.

---

[11] While the content analysis represents only 37 per cent of the submissions to the IAMs, it does cover all of the Banks, the entire geographic spread of development lending, all of the Banks' project loan portfolios, and the duration of the IAMs' existence. The content analysis also reflects and reinforces data that demonstrates the policies triggered by claimants across all submissions (for example, a grievance citing a lack of access to information will trigger the Banks' information disclosure policies (see Park 2019; Lewis 2012).

Section 5 then concludes the Element by reviewing how the IAM procedures are used by claimants, arguing that in general they do provide access to justice in environmental matters. They are used to air grievances over the lack of participation, the lack of access to information, and damage to nature. However, they do not necessarily provide remedies for harm through problem-solving, and much more research is needed to examine how compliance investigations contribute to redress or remedy for harm from international development. Despite the rise of IGMs globally, more work is needed to establish how they can be more effective at providing recourse for environmental and social harm.

2 International Grievance Mechanisms and Procedural Environmental Rights

The evolution of often-separate fights for international human rights and protecting the environment are increasingly converging towards a conception of environmental rights or using human rights for environmental protection (Turner et al. 2019: 2). This Section identifies the human rights and standards for protection upheld by IGMs, highlighting procedural environmental rights. Section 1 distinguishes the Guiding Principles for Business and Human Rights (GPs) in relation to Human Rights and Transnational Corporations and other Business Enterprises established by the UN Special Representative of the Secretary-General John Ruggie, compared with the standards set by the World Bank that have been emulated by other public and private funders. Section 2 details the criteria for IGMs to provide effective access to justice in environmental matters, and how this compares with our knowledge of their practices. Finally, Section 3 raises concerns that access to justice in environmental matters as practised by the IGMs places the onus on people to demonstrate harm which may not capture the full extent of environmental damage.

What Harms, What Rights? Standards of Protection for People and the Environment

IGMs are non-judicial mechanisms for providing access to justice for people who have or may face human rights abuses and environmental and social harm arising from the activities of transnational or international actors. They are triggered by complaints initiated by people, which distinguishes them from transnational accountability mechanisms set up to operate on behalf of affected people, such as international framework agreements between MNCs and trade unions (Zagelmeyer et al. 2018). Transnational accountability mechanisms may include initiatives for the private sector, supported by NGOs such as fair trade associations, the Fair Labor Association, and Rugmark. These operate on behalf of affected people and have mixed results, especially if they are private, market-based accountability systems that are influenced by consumer preferences (Keonig-Archibugi and Macdonald 2013, 2017; Partzsch 2020). Other IGMs may be company specific, such as for Adidas or Hewlett Packard; these are run voluntarily by the MNC and are difficult to examine in terms of their willingness to hear and respond to claims from people harmed at their site of operations (Lukas et al. 2016). The IGMs analysed here operate by placing the burden of proof with people being harmed being able to causally link an agent responsible to the harm in order to have the harm recognised and addressed (Mason 2005). While subsequent sections uncover whether access to justice in environmental matters is being met by the IAMs of the multilateral development banks, we first need to know exactly what environmental and social protection standards IGMs seek to uphold.

Two types of standards have emerged over time: first, standards for MNCs and business enterprises that have been solidified by the United Nations, which reference procedural environmental rights. Second, standards established by the World Bank and the MDBs that detail specific environmental protections, which have been subsequently adapted for private sector development financiers (Marcs 2019). The term 'standard' is

> used in the generic sense to encapsulate developments which provide detail relating to the level of protection that a regime provides, regardless of whether the authority from which they are derived actually refers to them as a 'standard' as such. Therefore, initiatives such as 'guidelines' have been included as they also provide an indication of the standard of protection that can be expected under a particular regime (Turner et al. 2019: 384).

Many protection standards are non-binding although they derive from international human rights law and environmental declarations; some even argue that the World Bank's standards constitute global administrative law (Kingsbury et al. 2005).[12]

UN Standards for Environmental and Social Protection for the Private Sector

In 2011, the UN Human Rights Council endorsed the Guiding Principles for Business and Human Rights in relation to human rights and transnational corporations and other business enterprises. The Guiding Principles in turn build upon the UN's work under the Global Compact from 2000 that attempted to harness the

---

[12] In signing a loan agreement with the World Bank, borrowers are contractually bound to adhere to the Bank's standards where appropriate.

global shift towards corporate social responsibility, where the activities of MNCs are considered to be best addressed by companies themselves. The Global Compact identifies ten principles that states, labour, civil society, and business can voluntarily adopt (Ruggie 2001). The principles are drawn from international customary laws and convention: the Universal Declaration of Human Rights, the International Labour Organization's (ILO) Declaration on Fundamental Principles and Rights at Work, the Rio Declaration on Environment and Development, and the United Nations Convention against Corruption. There are three specific environmental principles: Principle 7: that 'businesses should support a precautionary approach to environmental challenges;' Principle 8: that 'business undertake initiatives to promote greater environmental responsibility;' and Principle 9: that business should 'encourage the development and diffusion of environmentally friendly technologies' (UN Global Compact 2019). In 2003 the UN Sub-Commission on the Promotion and Protection of Human Rights approved the Norms on the Responsibilities of Transnational Corporations and other Business Enterprises (Resolution 2003/16) but they failed to gain traction (Ruggie 2013: 188).[13]

UN attempts to regulate transnational enterprises began in the 1970s. From 1975 to 1992, the UN Commission on Transnational Corporations (UNCTC) operated to negotiate a code of conduct for MNCs, which ultimately failed (Sagafi-Nejad and Dunning 2008). Instead, in 1976 the OECD established Guidelines on Multinational Enterprises, to 'promote responsible business conduct consistent with applicable laws' (Weissbrodt and Kruger, 2003: 902).[14] Other declarations also existed such as the 1977 ILO's 'Tripartite Declaration of Principles Concerning Multinational Enterprises, which calls upon businesses to follow the relevant ILO conventions and recommendations' (Weissbrot and Kuger 2003: 902–3). The OECD guidelines were updated in 2000, and again in 2011, this time incorporating the Guiding Principles (Ruggie and Nelson 2015). The 2011 OECD guidelines contain eight standards on the environment that reference the Rio Declaration Principle 15 (the precautionary approach), Agenda 21, and ISO standard on environmental management systems, while it 'takes into account' the Aarhus convention (OECD 2011: 44).[15]

There are three UN Guiding Principles: to protect, respect, and remedy human rights abuses. The first stipulates that *states* have responsibilities to protect against human rights abuses by business enterprises. This includes an obligation to

---

[13] The UN norms included an obligation for environmental protection in accordance with national laws and international agreements and standards (Resolution 2003/16, p. 6).

[14] OECD guidelines are recommendations for best practice for states. They included having a National Contact Point to address grievances arising from MNCs in states' territories.

[15] There are also sector specific OECD Guidelines.

'prevent, investigate, punish and redress such abuse through effective policies, legislation, regulations and adjudication' (UN 2011: 3). To do this, states must make clear that business enterprises must respect human rights and whether this is based on domestic law, domestic law with extraterritorial dimensions, multilateral soft-law such as the OECD's Multilateral Guideline for Multinational Enterprises, or 'performance standards required by institutions that support overseas investments' such as the World Bank standards and their permutations as outlined in the following (UN 2011: 4). People harmed by an MNC may take their complaint to the National Contact Point provided by their government if they live in a state that has signed the Multilateral Guideline for Multinational Enterprises. The Guidelines have been frequently reviewed and were strengthened after realising their vague and optional nature, while National Contact Points have significant discretion over their interpretation. The National Contact Point uses its good offices to attempt to address the grievance between the parties. The types of concerns being brought to the National Contact Points include the following: 'Displacement and forced eviction, compensation, employment conditions, living wages and workers' livelihoods, health and safety, human rights impacts following environmental damage, indigenous peoples' rights, the right to privacy, harassment, rape and use of force' (Lukas et al. 2016).

Second, *corporations* have responsibilities to respect human rights and address any human rights impacts of their activities. They must also seek to prevent or mitigate human rights impacts 'that are directly linked to their operations, products or services by their business relationships, even if they have not contributed to those impacts'. The principle refers to all rights detailed in the International Bill of Human Rights, comprised of the Universal Declaration of Human Rights, the International Covenant on Civil and Political Rights, and the International Covenant on Economic, Social and Cultural Rights. These are 'coupled with the principles concerning fundamental rights in the eight ILO core conventions as set out in the Declaration on Fundamental Principles and Rights at Work' and the additional UN human rights conventions and declarations covering women, Indigenous People, minorities, people with disabilities, children, and migrant workers and their families. Importantly, the 'severity of impacts will be judged by their scale, scope and irremediable character' (UN 2011: 14–15).

Third, *both* states and corporations should provide access to remedies when human rights are breached. State institutions for the provision of remedies may include: 'the courts (for both criminal and civil actions), labour tribunals, national human rights institutions, National Contact Points under the Guidelines for Multinational Enterprises of the Organisation for Economic Co-operation and Development, many ombudsperson offices, and Government-run complaints

offices.' For states and corporations, this may entail the use of IGMs or international or regional human rights bodies to provide recourse. Operational level
grievance mechanisms (such as at the factory or project site) can provide 'early
stage recourse and resolution' that may be nested within international and
regional human rights mechanisms. Operational level grievance mechanisms
must engage and consult with stakeholder groups using dialogue to address
grievances. In response to alleged crimes corporations must cooperate with
judicial mechanisms (UN 2011: 28, 34, 25).

There is little reference in the Guiding Principles as to how business impacts
on the environment, although procedural environmental rights are evident. To
enact human rights principles, business enterprises are expected to do the
following: first they must have a human rights policy that is publicly available
(access to information). Second, they should undertake due diligence including
risk assessments, and environmental and social impact assessments, and where
appropriate engage in 'meaningful consultation with potentially affected groups
and other relevant stakeholders' (UN 2011: 19–20). In other words, they must
provide access to participation. Finally, they must have legitimate processes of
remediation to address harm through, for example, an operation-level grievance
mechanism (access to justice in environmental matters). The Guiding Principles
do not reference free prior and informed consent, stating that business should
engage in consultation rather than gain consent from affected stakeholders.

World Bank Standards for Environmental and Social Protection

This section identifies the protection standards established by the World Bank
and emulated by other MDBs and private funders over time. The IAMs of the
multilateral development banks (see Table 2.1) address environmental and
social harm that has emerged because of the financing of international development projects including but not limited to energy, infrastructure, and natural
resource extraction. These mechanisms are triggered by affected people in
response to a failure by the Banks to uphold their environmental and social
protection standards. The World Bank first developed specific policies, guidelines, and procedures to protect people and the environment whilst financing
international development projects. All World Bank practices are governed by
the organisation's internal operational policies (OPs) which are derived, where
relevant, from the Bank's Articles of Agreement (its constitution). The operational policies cover activities including its business products, lending instruments, information disclosure, and social and environmental protection
measures. Specific standards evolved over time for ensuring information is
available, and that people can participate in development projects affecting

Table 2.1 World Bank Environmental and Social Safeguard Policies 1970s-2000s

Initial Environmental and Social Policies and Guidelines 1970-1980s	Institutionalised Safeguard Policies 1990s	Converted Safeguard Policies 2000-2009[1]	Environmental and Social Framework 2016 (and policies from 2010 onwards)
OMS2.36 Environmental Aspects of Bank Work (1984)	OD4.01 Environmental Assessment (1991; OD4.00 1989)	OP/BP4.01 Environmental Assessment (1991) OP/BP 4.00 Piloting the Use of Borrower Systems to Address Environmental and Social Safeguard Issues in Bank Supported Projects (new, 2005)	ESS1 Assessment and Management of Environmental and Social Risks and Impacts
OPN 11.02 Wildlands: Their Protection and Management in Economic Development (1986)	OD4.04 Natural Habitats (1995)	OP/BP4.04 Natural Habitats (2001)	ESS6 Biodiversity Conservation and Sustainable Management of Living Natural Resources
OPN11.01 Guidelines for the Selection and Use of Pesticides in Bank Financed Projects and their Procurement when Financed by the Bank (1985). Updated in 1987.	OD4.09 Pest Management (1996)	OP4.09 Pest Management (1998)	ESS3 Resource Efficiency and Pollution Prevention and Management

Table 2.1 (cont.)

Initial Environmental and Social Policies and Guidelines 1970-1980s	Institutionalised Safeguard Policies 1990s	Converted Safeguard Policies 2000-2009[1]	Environmental and Social Framework 2016 (and policies from 2010 onwards)
OMS2.33 Social Issues Associated with Involuntary Resettlement in Bank Financed Projects (1980). Updated in 1986 as OMS10.08 Operations Issues in the Treatment of Involuntary Resettlement in Bank Financed Projects.	OD4.30 Involuntary Resettlement (1990)	OP/BP4.12 Involuntary Resettlement (2001)	ESS5 Land Acquisition, Restrictions on Land Use and Involuntary Resettlement
OMS2.34 Tribal People in Bank Financed Projects (1982)	OD4.20 Indigenous People (1991)	OP/BP4.10 Indigenous People (2005)	ESS7 Indigenous Peoples/ Sub-Saharan African Historically Underserved Traditional Local Communities
Forestry Sector Policy Chapter (1978)	OP4.36 Forests (1993) and Forestry Strategy (1991)	OP/BP4.36 Forests Policy and Strategy (2002)	ESS6 Biodiversity Conservation and Sustainable Management

			of Living Natural Resources
OMS3.80 Safety of Dams (1977)	OP4.37 Safety of Dams (1996)	OP/BP4.37 Safety of Dams (2001)	ESS4 Community Health and Safety
OPN11.03 Management of Cultural Property in Bank Financed Projects (1986)	OD4.40/4.50 Draft Cultural Property (1991)	OP/BP4.11 Physical Cultural Property (2006)	ESS8 Cultural Heritage
OD7.50 Projects on International Waterways (1989)*	OP7.50 Projects on International Waterways (1994)	OP7.50 Projects on International Waterways (2001)	N/A
Not a Bank issue pre-1990s	OP7.60 Projects in Disputed Areas (1994)*	OP7.60 Projects in Disputed Areas (2001)	N/A
Not a Bank policy pre-2016	Not a Bank policy pre-2016	Not a Bank policy pre-2016	ESS2 Labor and Working Conditions
Not a Bank policy pre-2016	Not a Bank policy pre-2016	Not a Bank policy pre-2016	ESS10 Stakeholder Engagement and Information
Not a Bank issue pre-2016	Not a Bank issue pre-2016	Not a Bank issue pre-2016	ESS9 Financial Intermediaries

Table 2.1 (cont.)

Initial Environmental and Social Policies and Guidelines 1970-1980s	Institutionalised Safeguard Policies 1990s	Converted Safeguard Policies 2000-2009[1]	Environmental and Social Framework 2016 (and policies from 2010 onwards)
AMS 1.10 Directive on Disclosure of Information (1985)	BP17.50 Disclosure of Operational Information (1993)	World Bank Policy on Disclosure of Information (2002)	World Bank Access to Information Policy 2010 (revised 2013, 2015)

1 The safeguards policies were fully formalised in the 1990s as as mandatory Operational Directives (OD) from the previous advisory Operational Manual Statements (OMS), Operational Policy Notes (OPN), or Administrative Manual Statement (AMS). In the 2000s these were clarified as mandatory Operational Policies (OP) or guideline Bank Policies (BP) to determine in part, which of the policy was investigable by the Inspection Panel as being complied with. The dates in the fourth column refer to the shift to the Performance Standards which collapse some of the previous policies. The information disclosure policy remains separate and updated.

* Not discussed in this section.

them, along with protecting Indigenous Peoples, and stopping the forcible movement of people (see Table 2.1).

Despite this, the World Bank has no comprehensive human rights policy (Sarfaty 2009; Fujita 2013). The MDBs more broadly resist discussing social protection standards as human rights on the basis that their Articles of Agreement preclude political interference in their member states' activities (Clapham 2006). In 2015, the UN Special Rapporteur on Extreme Poverty, Philip Alston, stated that the World Bank treats 'human rights more like an infectious disease than universal values and obligations' because of its 'anachronistic and inconsistent interpretation of the 'political prohibition' contained in its Articles of Agreement' (UN 2015: 20, para 68). This is despite criticism that they are subject to human rights obligations under international law (Darrow 2003), and the identification of the harm World Bank policies can have (Abouhard and Cingranelli 2007).

The protection standards emerged within the World Bank in prelude to the 1972 UN Conference on the Human Environment. The World Bank's policies expanded during the 1980s as transnational environmental campaigns revealed how its development projects contributed to environmental and human harm (Clark et al. 2003; Fox and Brown 1998), while the spotlight remained focused on international cooperation through the 1987 Bruntland Report and in preparation for the UN Conference on Environment and Development in 1992. By the late 1990s, the World Bank had a suite of safeguard policies in place (see Table 2.1). Environmental Assessment (EA) is the overarching policy for the remaining environmental and social policies because it assesses the extent to which a project requires oversight. Each project goes through a screening process to determine the type and depth of EA required, and which of the safeguards apply. The application of the Environmental Assessment depends on whether the project is classified as a high environmental and social risk (category A), less risky (B), no risk (C), or pertaining to a project undertaken by a financial intermediary (FI). The safeguards are operational policies that are incorporated into borrowers' project loan agreements where required. The standards were institutionalised within the World Bank through the project cycle (the main vehicle for project lending) backed by monitoring and evaluation procedures.

From 1994, the World Bank would be held to account for meeting its protection standards by the Inspection Panel.[16] This meant that people affected by a project financed by the World Bank could submit a claim for recourse for harm under the Inspection Panel. For example, the Inspection Panel's very first investigation in 1994 found that the World Bank had not met

---

[16] This section, unless otherwise stated, is from Park 2010.

its own policies on Environmental Assessment, Involuntary Resettlement, and Indigenous Peoples in relation to a claim submitted by two local NGOs in relation to the Arun III hydroelectric project in Nepal (Park 2019). The controversy led then-President of the World Bank James Wolfensohn to cancel the loan.

The safeguards are recognised benchmarks for how to mitigate negative environmental and social impacts by the World Bank; by its borrowers and contractors; and by other MDBs, including the World Bank Group (see Table 2.2). This means that most of the international development financiers follow similar policies when considering the need to move people, or whether Indigenous Peoples will be affected, or whether local biodiversity will be irreparably harmed, when devising development projects like dams, mines, railways, and roads. Moreover, the other MDBs standards revert to the more detailed World Bank standards where gaps remain.

From 2003, the IFC's standards, themselves adapted from the World Bank, would be translated into the Equator Principles for private sector financiers to manage their environmental and social risk in international project finance (see Table 2.4; Hunter 2008: 450). In 2006, the IFC reworked its safeguard policies that it had adopted from the World Bank into a sustainability framework with performance standards. This translated external policies to hold the companies it lends and invests in to account, into an internal risk management framework for companies to use themselves (Wright 2007). This led IFC to include labour protections for the first time (see Table 2.3). IFC's most recent performance standards recognise that business must respect human rights in accordance with the Guiding Principles, and explicitly adopted free, prior and informed consent for Indigenous Peoples in accordance with UNDRIP (IFC 2012: 5, 22; Razzaque 2019: 204). IFC has explicitly stated that human rights can be addressed through its environmental and social standards (IFC 2012b: 1; Mares 2019: 523).

After years of deliberation, in 2016, the World Bank established an Environmental and Social Framework which came into effect in 2018. The Environmental and Social Framework, like the IFC's Sustainability Framework, seeks to provide a risk management framework for borrower states to have ownership over their own development. This was mandated by the Bank's board to increase their coverage and harmonisation across the World Bank Group, to improve supervision and monitoring, and to 'improve accountability and grievance redress systems and instruments' (World Bank 2016). NGOs have countered this by arguing the Environmental and Social Framework has loopholes that allow the Bank to avoid environmental and social protections (CIEL, 2016), which may enable more opposition from Bank management and borrowers to the Inspection Panel (Passoni et al., 2016).

Table 2.2 Current environmental and social protection standards of the Multilateral Development Banks

MDB Policy	AfDB Integrated Safeguards System (2013)	ADB Safeguard Policy (SPS 2013)	EBRD Environmental and Social Policy (2014)	IDB
Umbrella Environmental and Social Policy	OS 1: Environmental and Social Assessment	OM Section C3 Incorporation of Social Dimensions into ADB Operations (2010) SPS Requirement 1 Environmental	PR 1: Assessment and Management of Environmental and Social Impacts and Issues	OP 703: Environment and Safeguards Compliance (2006)
Involuntary Resettlement	OS 2: Involuntary Resettlement: Land Acquisition, Population Displacement and Compensation	SPS Requirement 2 Involuntary Resettlement	PR 5: Land Acquisition, Involuntary Resettlement and Economic Displacement	OP 710: Involuntary Resettlement (1998)
Indigenous Peoples		SPS Requirement 3 Indigenous Peoples	PR 7: Indigenous Peoples	OP 765: Indigenous Peoples (2006)
Gender and Development		OM Section C2 Gender and Development (2010)		OP 761: Gender Equality in Development (2010)

Table 2.2 (cont.)

MDB Policy	AfDB Integrated Safeguards System (2013)	ADB Safeguard Policy (SPS 2013)	EBRD Environmental and Social Policy (2014)	IDB
Physical Cultural Resources			PR 8: Cultural Heritage	
Natural Habitats	OS 3: Biodiversity and Ecosystem Services		PR 6: Biodiversity Conservation and Sustainable Management of Living Natural Resources	
Poverty Reduction		OM Section C1 Poverty Reduction (2004)		
Information	Disclosure and Access to Information (2012) Policy and Guidelines on Cooperation with Civil Society Organizations (2000)	Access to Information Policy (2019)	PR 10: Information Disclosure and Stakeholder Engagement Access to Information Policy (2019)	OP 102 Access to Information (2010)
Energy Sector	Energy Sector Policy 2011	Energy Policy (2009)		

Resource Efficiency and Pollution Prevention	OS 4: Pollution Prevention and Control, Greenhouse Gases, Hazardous Materials and Resource Efficiency	PR 3: Resource Efficiency and Pollution Prevention and Control	
Labour	OS 5: Labour Conditions, Health and Safety	PR 2: Labour and Working Conditions	
Community Health, Safety and Security	OS 5: Labour Conditions, Health and Safety	PR 4: Health and Safety	
Disaster Risk Management			OP 704: Natural Disaster Risk Management (2007)
Financial Intermediaries		PR 8: Financial Intermediaries	

Table 2.3 International Finance Corporation Environmental and Social
Policies, 1998–2012

IFC's 1998 Environmental and Social Safeguard Policies adapted from the World Bank's Safeguards	IFC's Policy and Performance Standards on Environmental and Social Sustainability Effective 30 April 2006	IFC's Policy and Performance Standards on Environmental and Social Sustainability Effective January 1 2012
OP 4.01 Environmental Assessment (policy devised 1998)	Performance standard 1: Social and Environmental Assessment Management System	Performance standard 1: Assessment and Management of Environmental and Social Risks and Impacts
OP 4.04 Natural Habitats (1998)	Performance standard 6: Biodiversity Conservation and Sustainable Natural Resource Management	Performance standard 6: Biodiversity Conservation and Sustainable Management of Natural Living Resources
OP 4.36 Forestry (1998)	Performance standard 6: Biodiversity Conservation and Sustainable Natural Resource Management	Performance standard 6: Biodiversity Conservation and Sustainable Management of Natural Living Resources
OP 4.09 Pest Management (1998)	Performance standard 6: Biodiversity Conservation and Sustainable Natural Resource Management Performance standard 3: Pollution Prevention and Abatement	Performance standard 6: Biodiversity Conservation and Sustainable Natural Resource Management Performance standard 3: Resource Efficiency and Pollution Prevention
OP 7.50 International Waterways (1998)	N/A	N/A

Table 2.3 (cont.)

IFC's 1998 Environmental and Social Safeguard Policies adapted from the World Bank's Safeguards	IFC's Policy and Performance Standards on Environmental and Social Sustainability Effective 30 April 2006	IFC's Policy and Performance Standards on Environmental and Social Sustainability Effective January 1 2012
OD 4.30 Involuntary Resettlement (adapted from the World Bank's 1990 policy)	Performance standard 5: Land Acquisition and Involuntary Resettlement	Performance standard 5: Land Acquisition and Involuntary Resettlement
OD 4.20 Indigenous People (1991 policy)	Performance standard 7: Indigenous People	Performance standard 7: Indigenous People
OP 4.37 Safety on Dams (1996 policy)	Performance standard 4: Community Health, Safety and Security	Performance standard 4: Community Health, Safety and Security
OPN 11.03 Cultural Property (1986 policy)	Performance standard 8: Cultural Heritage	Performance standard 8: Cultural Heritage
Policy Statement on Child Labour and Forced Labour (1998) – unique to IFC	Performance standard 2: Labour and Working Conditions	Performance standard 2: Labour and Working Conditions
Policy on Disclosure of Information (1998)	Policy on Disclosure of Information (2006)	Access to Information Policy (2012)

Mares (2019) argues for further cross-fertilisation among the Guiding Principles, World Bank, and IFC standards to protect human rights, although it is clear that it is already occurring: the World Bank has flagged its objective to respect human rights, including the adoption of free, prior and informed consent in the Environmental and Social Framework in 2016 in relation to Indigenous Peoples (World Bank 2016: 76). This means that Indigenous People must consent for their land to be used for development projects. Previously, it had only required borrowers to 'engage in a process of free, prior, and informed consultation' (Razzaque 2019: 205; World Bank OP4.10). The World Bank (2016), IFC (2012), the Equator

Table 2.4 The Equator Principles for Private Sector Development Financiers, 2003–2013[17]

Equator Principles (June 2003)	Equator Principles II (June 2006)	Equator Principles (June 2013)
1. 'We have categorised the risk of a project in accordance with internal guidelines based upon the environmental and social screening criteria of the IFC as described in the attachment to these Principles' (Review and categorisation)	1. Review and categorisation	1. Review and categorisation
2. 'For all Category A and Category B projects, the borrower has completed an Environmental Assessment (EA), the preparation of which is consistent with the outcome of our categorisation process and addresses to our satisfaction key environmental and social issues identified during the categorisation process' (Environmental assessment)	2. Social and environmental assessment – key diff from 1 to 2: 'EA' becomes ESIA	2. Environmental and social assessment – introduced alternatives analysis too
3. '… the EA report has addressed a) assessment of baseline environmental and social conditions	3. Applicable social and environmental standards	3. Applicable environmental and social standards – min standard IFC Performance Standards

[17] Equator Principles (2003) *Equator Principles: An industry approach for financial institutions in determining, assessing and managing environmental & social risk in project financing.* June; Equator Principles (2006) *Equator Principles: An industry approach for financial institutions in determining, assessing and managing environmental & social risk in project financing.* June. https://equator-principles.com/best-practice-resources/; Equator Principles (2013) *Equator Principles: An industry approach for financial institutions in determining, assessing and managing environmental & social risk in project financing.* June. https://equator-principles.com /best-practice-resources/

Table 2.4 (cont.)

Equator Principles (June 2003)	Equator Principles II (June 2006)	Equator Principles (June 2013)
b) host country requirements c) sustainable development and use of renewable natural resources d) protection of human health, biodiversity, endangered species and sensitive ecosystems e) use of dangerous substances f) major hazards g) OHS h) fire prevention and life safety i) socioeconomic impacts j) land acquisition and use k) involuntary resettlement l) impacts on indigenous communities m) cumulative impacts n) participation of affected parties o) consideration of alternatives p) energy efficiency q) pollution' (Applicable social and environmental standards) – min standard: WB and IFC Pollution Prevention + Abatement Guidelines; WB Indicators Database; IFC Safeguard Policies	– min standard: IFC Performance Standards (2006–2012) and EHS Guidelines	(2013>) and EHS Guidelines
4. 'For all Category A projects, and as considered appropriate for Category B projects, the borrower or third party expert has prepared an Environmental Management Plan (EMP) which draws on	4. Action plan and management system	4. Environmental and social management system and Equator Principles action plan

Table 2.4 (cont.)

Equator Principles (June 2003)	Equator Principles II (June 2006)	Equator Principles (June 2013)
the conclusions of the EA. The EMP has addressed mitigation, action plans, monitoring, management of risk and schedules' (Action plan and management system)		
5. 'For all Category A projects and, as considered appropriate for Category B projects, we are satisfied that the borrower or third party expert has consulted, in a structured and culturally appropriate way, with project affected groups, including indigenous peoples and local NGOs. The EA, or a summary thereof, has been made available to the public for a reasonable minimum period in local language and in a culturally appropriate manner. The EA and the EMP will take account of such consultations, and for Category A Projects, will be subject to independent expert review' (Consultation and disclosure and independent review)	5. Consultation and disclosure	5. Stakeholder engagement – main diff includes 'This process should be free from external manipulation, interference, coercion and intimidation' – + paragraph about indigenous people
6. 'The borrower has covenanted to:	6. Grievance mechanism	6. Grievance mechanism – addition of 'without retribution to the party that

Table 2.4 (cont.)

Equator Principles (June 2003)	Equator Principles II (June 2006)	Equator Principles (June 2013)
a) comply with the EMP in the construction and operation of the project b) provide regular reports, prepared by in-house staff or third party experts, on compliance with the EMP c) where applicable, decommission the facilities in accordance with an agreed Decommissioning Plan' (Covenants)		originated the issue or concern. The mechanism should not impede access to judicial or administrative remedies.'
7. 'As necessary, lenders have appointed an independent environmental expert to provide additional monitoring and reporting services' (Independent monitoring and reporting)	7. Independent review	7. Independent review
8. 'In circumstances where a borrower is not in compliance with its environmental and social covenants, such that any debt financing would be in default, we will engage the borrower in its efforts to seek solutions to bring it back into compliance with its covenants' (part of Covenants in 2006)	8. Covenants – main diff is the addition of 'comply with all relevant host country social and environmental laws' – 'bring back into compliance' (8 in 2003) included here	8. Covenants – main diff is removal of 'to comply with all relevant host country social and environmental laws, regulations and permits in all material respect'
9. 'These principles apply to projects with a total capital cost of $50 million or more'	9. Independent monitoring and reporting	9. Independent monitoring and reporting

Table 2.4 (cont.)

Equator Principles (June 2003)	Equator Principles II (June 2006)	Equator Principles (June 2013)
	10. Equator Principles Financial Institutions (EPFI) reporting	10. Reporting and transparency – Addition of two client reporting requirements – ESIA placed online – Addition of two client reporting requirements – client will publicly report GHG emission levels

Principles (2013) and UNDRIP now align on free, prior and informed consent, while the Guiding Principles more generally defer to 'performance standards required by institutions that support overseas investments' such as those outlined here, and use a due diligence approach that accords with environmental and social risk management used by the development financiers (Mares 2019: 521; UN 2011: 4).[18] Both the IFC (2006, 2012) and the World Bank (2018) also now include labour standards, as does the African Development Bank and the European Bank for Reconstruction and Development (see Table 2.2).

In sum, procedural environmental rights emerged within the World Bank and other development lenders over time: access to information is provided for in the form of information disclosure policies. Access to participation is referenced in relation to meaningful consultation in environmental assessment policies, as well as in specific policies on poverty reduction, gender dimensions of development, involuntary resettlement, Indigenous People (World Bank 1993: Annex I), and the later incorporation of free, prior and informed consent. Access to justice in environmental matters is evident in the creation of the IAMs from 1994 onward (see Table 2.5). The following section details how IGMs seek to uphold these standards.

What Obligations? IGMs and Procedural Rights

This section details how the IGMs provide justice in environmental matters in terms of their criteria for effectiveness, their operations, and their dependence on claimants to provide evidence of harm occurring, which may overlook some types

---

[18] The OECD also follows free, prior and informed consent (OECD 2017).

Table 2.5 The Accountability Mechanisms of the MDBs: Iterations and Updates of their Resolutions and Rules of Practice (updated from Park 2017).

MDB	First Iteration of the Accountability Mechanism	Second Iteration
World Bank	Inspection Panel 1994; clarified 1996	Inspection Panel 1999. Updated 2014. Updated 2020 to include a Dispute Resolution Service
Inter-American Development Bank	Independent Investigation Mechanism (IIM) 1994–2009	Independent Consultation and Investigation Mechanism (ICIM/ MICI), 2010. Updated 2014.
Asian Development Bank	Inspection Function 1995–2002	Accountability Mechanism (AM) 2003. Updated 2012.
World Bank Group (IFC/MIGA)	Compliance Advisor/ Ombudsman (CAO) 1999. Updated 2007 and 2013.	N/A
European Bank for Reconstruction and Development	Independent Recourse Mechanism (IRM) 2003–2008	Project Complaint Mechanism (PCM) 2009. Updated 2014. *Third Iteration: Independent Project Accountability Mechanism (effective 2020)*
African Development Bank	Independent Review Mechanism (IRM) 2004. Updated 2015.	N/A

of environmental destruction. IGMs seek to provide a non-judicial means for recourse in accordance with the rights and protection standards as previously outlined. Given the voluntary nature of the IGMs, they are unable to force compliance by the company or financial institution. Underlying this is that the Guiding Principles, while derived from international law, view the 'responsibility to respect human rights as a "global standard of expected conduct"' or as a social expectation for companies. This raises the question as to which responsibilities for human rights are optional (Bilchitz and Deva 2013: 13)? It also raises the issue of attempting to reconcile objective human rights to the subjective preferences of the parties in remediation (Thompson 2017). Dissatisfaction from communities with corporate driven IGMs highlight both of these concerns when the IGMs fail to resolve the grievance, fail to meet international standards for the provision of a remedy, fail to provide a remedy, or provide a culturally inappropriate remedy (Kaufman and McDonnell 2015: 129). Although the IAMs of the MDBs have the capacity to undertake mediation or compliance investigations (outlined in Sections 3 and 4), until recently most did not have the power to oversee whether the Banks were implementing their recommendations for remedy.

Over time, criteria have emerged for how IGMs should operate to provide access to justice. The Guiding Principles state quite clearly that IGMs must have 'impartiality, integrity, and ability to accord due process' (UN 2011: 28). The Guiding Principles outline effective IGMs as being legitimate, accessible, predictable, equitable, transparent, rights-compatible, and a source of continuous learning (UN 2011: 33–4). These paralleled criteria determined by the IAMs of the MDBs that they should be accessible, credible, efficient, and effective (Inspection Panel 2009: Annex B, 109–12). Soon after the Guiding Principles were endorsed, the IAMs of the MDBs reframed their criteria in 2012 to act with integrity and be accessible, transparent, independent, impartial, professional, and responsive (Lewis 2012). To date, of the MDB IAMs, only the World Bank Group's CAO and the Inter-American Development Bank's Independent Consultation and Investigation Mechanism (known by its Spanish acronym MICI) reference the Guiding Principles (CAO 2018; ICIM 2011). Although the Inspection Panel has stated that the World Bank ought to recognise human rights (Schmitt 2017: 216; Inspection Panel 2009), it has 'remained conspicuously silent when Requestors specifically claimed violations of international law' (Naude Fourie 2012: 231).

The IAMs' criteria are commensurate with the UN Guiding Principles.[19] First, the mechanisms and the process for a complaint should be accessible in terms of people being aware of the process, and people should be able to reasonably file a request, and affected people should have the capacity to file a claim. Second, the process for a complaint should be credible in terms of being conducted independently from the company or Bank management and

---

[19] Both criteria have overlaps with the Aarhus Convention which states that access to justice in environmental matters includes: 'access to judicial or administrative procedures to challenge acts and omissions by private persons and public authorities', the provision of adequate and effective remedies, and be fair, equitable, timely, and not prohibitively expensive (Aarhus 1998: Article 9, para 3–5). IGMs on the whole are silent on the provision of adequate and effective remedies as well as the cost to complainants for submitting claims.

operations; they should be impartial to all actors involved; treat all participants and information with integrity; and undertake the investigation competently and as transparently as possible. The Guiding Principles criteria also adds that the process should be legitimate in terms of all parties accepting its authority, that it should act predictably to ensure credibility and to provide procedural justice. Third, the IGMs should be efficient in terms of timeliness and resources used to expeditiously respond to community grievances. Finally, the accountability mechanisms should be responsive to claimants, and in taking and conveying information to the company or Bank. The Guiding Principles criteria also states that IGMs should be rights compatible to ensure that human rights are not violated during the process or as a result of its decision-making, and that it should be a source for continuous learning for the company or Bank to improve its operations over time. In the 2012 version of the criteria the IAMs dropped effectiveness, because they viewed effectiveness as meeting the other criteria (accessible, transparent, independent, impartial, acting with integrity, and being professional and responsive; Lewis 2012).[20]

A recent study by Zagelmeyer et al. (2018) reviewed the operations of existing IGMs to ascertain their structure, coverage, procedures, outcomes, and effectiveness in relation to the Guiding Principles criteria. Many IGMs focus on human rights and conditions of work compared with environmental matters. While there is a variety of structures and coverage, there was uncertainty over which IGM procedures existed, and no evidence of how decisions for remedy are made, implemented, and enforced, or how management incorporate feedback and learning (Zagelmeyer et al. 2018: 24–5). The review highlights the dearth of publicly available information on IGMs established by corporations, with limited and primarily case study research conducted predominantly by NGOs. The results of the report point to a glaring lacuna on the procedural or substantive practices of corporations in using IGMs either alone or as part of multi-stakeholder processes. One exception finds that IGMs are over-reliant on monetary compensation as a remedy, while being unable to adequately address human rights concerns compared with judicial mechanisms (Lukas et al. 2016: 326–8).

In comparison, the operations of existing IAMs are relatively well documented, with all the ones examined here having public online case registries. They clearly detail their coverage and procedures and most provide a template for complainants to use to meet their procedural criteria (making them relatively accessible). They provide updates on where in the process the complaint is,

---

[20] The Inspection Panel viewed its effectiveness on the basis of the claimant, host government, and Bank benefiting from the process, although arguably this was beyond the remit of the Inspection Panel to assess (Inspection Panel 2009: Annex B: 111–12).

making them transparent. While some, like the CAO, accept anonymity, the outcomes are accessible in the documents provided and in summary form where confidential, although the IAMs vary with their timeliness in providing updates on the cases and their outcomes (Park 2019). An NGO review of their operational effectiveness argued that less than half of the claims submitted to the IAMs were deemed eligible, while only 20 per cent led to a successful mediation or a complete compliance investigation report (Huijstee et al. 2016).[21] The effectiveness of the IAMs in addressing grievances through problem-solving or compliance investigation are detailed in the following sections.[22]

For now, it is important to highlight two issues: First, IGMs tend to hew either to the UN Guiding Principles, the World Bank protection standards, or sector-specific international framework agreements for non-judicial access to justice internationally. As outlined previously, the Guiding Principles and the World Bank standards are moving closer together, creating a dense web of human rights and environmental standards. Criteria for how the IGMs should operate have also been established, with Guiding Principles efforts and those of the IAMs of the MDBs emerging in parallel, with some overlaps as to what constitutes access to justice. However, there is little evidence of ascertaining whether they do what they were created to do. Sections 3 and 4 seek to identify how the IAMs of the MDBs provide access to justice in environmental matters and rectify breaches of environmental procedural rights such as access to information and participation, with an additional analysis on the rights of nature.

The second concern, and this will be examined throughout the following sections, is how IGMs operate in practice, and whether they do provide access to justice in environmental matters in ways that address environmental harm. As noted earlier in the section, many of the IGMs established focus on human rights abuses, less so procedural environmental rights, although they are evident in the Guiding Principles. Procedural environmental rights are also evident in the protection standards of the World Bank, other MDBs, and private development lenders. However, this may not be enough to ensure the integrity of ecosystems because the focus is on ensuring human rights and social protection rather than what is increasingly being understood as the rights of nature. These 'rights' include the right to exist, to regenerate, and to be restored when damaged (Kauffman and Sheehan 2019). Arguably, the integrity of ecosystems is covered through the standards such as environmental assessments. However, EAs are

---

[21] This study included bilateral export credit agencies.

[22] Although the reviews of the IAMs are conducted by the Banks or by independent consultants, most do not reference the IAMs own criteria for effective access to justice. Moreover, they do not evaluate whether people are better off after a claim.

predicated on the determination of what constitutes the project area. This can have significant ramifications. For example, where a project is assessed individually rather than considering series of projects for an area's development (even when the MDB is aware of, or preparing, other proposed projects nearby). Cumulatively, this can radically alter the environmental impact of a development on an ecosystem, possibly irreparably. While there are specific World Bank environmental protection standards (and permutations thereof), an assessment of how frequently they are triggered and addressed is still to be done.

Conclusion

This section outlined how IGMs operate by referencing the UN Guiding Principles or the World Bank protection standards as the basis for their attempts to provide access to justice in environmental matters. The section outlined the evolution of the Guiding Principles and the World Bank's standards and how they include procedural environmental rights even if they do not explicitly frame them as such. It also revealed a lack of information on how the IGMs were meeting their aims to provide access to justice, and the detailed criteria for how IGMs should operate as established by the UN and the IAMs of the MDBs in parallel. The final point of the section, and one that follows through the remaining sections, is the extent to which community demands for access to justice in environmental matters can be achieved through the IAMs of the MDBs, and whether this adequately covers the rights of nature, including, as well as beyond, the needs of people.

3 Access to Justice in Environmental Matters through the Problem-Solving Practices of the Independent Accountability Mechanisms of the MDBs

This section opens the discussion of how the IAMs can best advance access to justice in environmental matters through providing recourse for environmental and social harm. The focus here is the problem-solving processes of the IAMs, which seeks to provide consultation, mediation, dialogue, conciliation, and dispute resolution to redress the grievance. Aside from the World Bank Inspection Panel, which is excluded from the analysis in this section, all the other IAMs provide problem-solving in addition to their compliance investigation functions. Little has been written on the problem-solving processes of the IAMs, compared with the compliance investigations of the World Bank Inspection Panel, for example (the exception is Balaton-Chrimes and Haines 2015; for a discussion see Naude Fourie 2015). Over time, the IAMs have shifted towards allowing complainants to choose if they want their compliant to go to through the problem-solving process or if they want to trigger a compliance investigation (Park 2017). As mentioned previously, the initial IAMs for the Asian and Inter-American Development Banks and the World Bank Group required claimants to first go through problem-solving before being able to access the compliance investigation process, even if this is not what they wanted.[23]

By extracting evidence from a database of all of the cases submitted to the IAMs of the MDBs (Park 2019), which is derived from the public IAM case registries and annual reports, the section details how access to justice in environmental matters is possible, although it is narrowly conceived.[24] First, the section details what problem-solving is, and how the process operates. Claims are submitted to the IAMs: they are registered based on an initial assessment as to their validity; they are then assessed as to their eligibility; and all stakeholders must then agree to undertake problem-solving. The problem-solving initiative is then undertaken and a settlement may be facilitated. The process may then be concluded with an agreement among the parties, which the IAM monitors before closing the complaint. Next, the section analyses how environmental harm is conceived by claimants, in reference to themselves (access to information and participation) or to the right of nature to exist, to regenerate, and to be restored when damaged. This is based on a content analysis of the original public claims submitted by people to the IAMs, a total of 394 claims up to the end of 2018. Many of the claims are confidential and are therefore not available. Coding of the claims was undertaken to identify if they mentioned in their grievance lack of information, participation, or concern for the environment that was not linked to their own needs. Further detail of the coding is detailed in the third part of the section. The final part of the section presents data on what happens to people's claims as they progress through the problem-solving process, paying attention to whether claimants' reference procedural environmental rights such as a lack of access to information and participation.[25]

---

[23] Such as the ADB and IDB's mechanisms.

[24] The publicly available database (Park 2019) classifies the justifications the IAMs make for rejecting claims for registration and eligibility for problem-solving and compliance investigations. All discussion of criteria and justifications in the next two sections are drawn from the database and are detailed here.

[25] The Element does not detail how each of the Banks IAMs specifically undertake their activities as this is detailed elsewhere (Park unpublished).

What Is Problem-Solving?

The IAMs of the MDBs are 'last resorts' for people affected by MDB-financed projects. They are part of the internal accountability processes of the Banks to check their behaviour, meaning that any remedy agreed upon with stakeholders is dependent on being enacted by Bank management. Last resort means that grievances must first be directed towards the Bank's operations staff managing the project. If the operations department fails to respond to grievances adequately and in a timely manner, people may then take their concerns to Bank management or may submit a complaint to the IAM. The IAM can undertake 'problem-solving', meaning that it can directly engage with the claimants and the host government or project sponsor to solve the problem. Forms of redress may include preventing a project from going ahead or stopping a project already underway; altering a project to take affected people's concerns into account; making a project compliant with environmental and social standards; or providing compensation or services that enable a return to basic living standards.[26] The Banks aim to improve the conditions of affected people to pre-project levels (as per the World Bank and ADB's Involuntary Resettlement policies). While this is not always possible, a claim to the IAM can still make a difference to vulnerable communities through providing recourse leading to some form of redress (Park 2015).

Of course, rectifying the damage caused by a project may not be possible, which necessarily limits the ability of the IAM to provide remedies to people. This may be so for five reasons. First, a request for problem-solving does not stop the project from continuing, meaning that as problem-solving is underway the project may continue to contribute to harm. Second, a request may be submitted at any time throughout the project design or implementation stages (in some cases up to two years after a project has been completed). However, the later the request for problem-solving, the fewer remedies may be available as environmental damage may not be rectifiable or a return to previous livelihoods may be impossible. Therefore, a claim may improve people's material existence compared with conditions prior to the claim but it may not be commensurate with conditions prior to the project.

Third, problem-solving is at the behest of the Bank meaning that the IAMs may preclude some options that requestors want, including demanding immediate project changes, stopping the project altogether (the threshold for cancelling a project is high but not impossible, Park 2015), or substantially changing the project such as its location or design. In short, there are limits to how far

---

[26] The Bank itself does not offer compensation but may review whether the project sponsor or host government compensation to claimants met market value or protection standards.

people can hold the Banks to account for damaging behaviour through using IAMs, and problem-solving in particular. Fourth, a claim for problem-solving may be limited depending on how late the claim is submitted in relation to a project but for a different reason than those already given. The later the claim, the more likely that tensions between stakeholders may prevent problem-solving being possible. In other words, mediation may not be viable where relations between stakeholders have become toxic. Finally, many of the MDBs engage in financing private sector development activities in developing states (the ADB, the EBRD, the IDB, and the World Bank Group). This means relying on the willingness of the project sponsor (corporation) to engage in voluntary problem-solving, which may not be forthcoming.

For example, three claims were submitted to the European Bank for Reconstruction and Development's IAM in 2011 regarding inadequate safe-guards in the environmental impact assessment for a railway bypass in the capital of Georgia, Tbilisi. Georgian environmental NGO, Green Alternative, submitted one claim, with another representing ten families, and another sub-mitted by a local resident. They were concerned about the inadequate consult-ation and safeguards regarding the impact of the railway bypass, which was to be used to transport freight including oil, near local inhabitants, the Tbilisi national park, and one of its reservoirs for drinking water. Yet the claims were rejected for problem-solving because the company, Georgia Railway, withdrew their request for Bank funding. This meant that problem-solving was not therefore possible (EBRD 2012).

The IAMs adopted a similar informal practice of 'registering' claims that meet specific criteria. The process for problem-solving begins with registering bona fide claims. The IAMs all now have an online public registry of complaints submitted to the IAMs. This is the eligibility phase, which includes meeting the following criteria:

- the claim is about a project financed by the MDB;
- the claim concerns the environmental and social impacts of the project, excluding concerns regarding ethics, procurement, fraud, or corruption;
- claimants have already tried to seek a response from Bank management;
- the claim is from two or more people in the project affected area or from non-government organisations (NGOs) that have been designated representatives (except for the EBRD, where both individuals and NGOs may make claims);
- the project loan is still being disbursed (or in some cases the loan has already met a specified disbursement threshold such as two years after full disbursement);
- the project will be, has been, or is being implemented;

- the claim indicates evidence of harm;
- the claim references policies the Bank may not have complied with leading to the harm (some of the early IAMs made this compulsory, but most now recommend it);
- the project is not a subject of legal action, even if this is not by the claimants of affects claimants' concerns (for the African and Inter-American Development Banks, the European Bank for Reconstruction and Development, and World Bank).

To make claims more likely to be accepted for registration, the Banks now provide templates for claimants as to how to make a complaint. Once the IAM is satisfied that the criteria for registration has been met, the claim is registered. The IAMs then undertake a second stage, a formal assessment as to the claims eligibility for problem-solving, compliance investigation, or both. This is the assessment phase. As mentioned, early versions of some of the IAMs forced complainants to engage in problem-solving even if they did not want to, in order trigger a compliance investigation, while the mechanisms created later for the European Bank for Reconstruction and Development and the African Development Bank generally assessed whether problem-solving would be appropriate first. It might seem common sense that problem-solving to address grievances would be a better and therefore first option for addressing people's concerns. However, some claims are triggered by the Banks' failure to follow their environmental and social assessment standards, where corrections could be easily identified and rectified through a compliance investigation. This was the case in the claim by environmental professionals regarding the Bujagali dam in Uganda as mentioned in Section 1.

The following criteria are used, in addition to the aforementioned eligibility phase criteria (which may be reassessed), to assess the eligibility of a claim for problem-solving:

- there is reason to believe that the harm is being caused by the project because of Bank's acts or omissions;
- there are not already actions underway by Bank management to address claimants' grievances;
- the claim raises substantial concerns regarding environmental and social outcomes that would warrant an investigation;
- stakeholders must be willing to engage in a collaborative consultation process;
- the IAM believes it could play a useful role and can help the parties reach full agreement;
- the grievance is still a concern and can be verified.

In the assessment phase, the limits to access to justice in environmental matters becomes apparent in five ways. First, notably for the IAM process, there must be a link between the environmental and social harm caused by the acts or omissions of the Banks in complying with their environmental and social protection standards. If there is harm, but not linked to the Banks' acts or omissions, then there is no means for recourse through the IAMs. In other words, the IAMs cannot be used to address grievances for harms not caused by the Banks, even if the project has caused harm and financing the project has facilitated it.

Second, the IAMs have identified the limits to the substantive nature of the grievance that they will accept. Claims may therefore be rejected if the IAM believes that an investigation would yield limited information and/or be of limited value. The claim might be accepted if the grievance raises issues of systemic importance to how the Bank undertakes its operations, or if the claim raises substantial enough concerns regarding environmental and social out-comes to warrant an investigation. In other words, it may choose not to accept a grievance that is valid on the basis that is not a systemic issue for the Bank (regarding repeat violations of specific environmental and social protection standard, for example). This gives the IAMs discretion in terms of the claims it accepts. It also raises questions as to whether claims may go ignored if they are by a smaller number of people or for a grievance considered less of a concern for the Bank because it does not shine a light on repeatedly poor practices. For example, some claims may be made by two individuals, others by hundreds or thousands of claimants, or an issue might be considered an isolated 'offense' by the Bank. Again, the IAMs have discretion to use this not to undertake problem-solving (or a compliance investigation also).

Third, there is also discretion as to whether the IAM believes it could play a useful role in providing problem-solving, or whether it actually could help the parties reach full agreement. This justification is used in cases where the parties have reached some agreement but not been able to address all the grievances. It is also invoked where the parties have been unable to agree to proceed with problem-solving, either from the claimant, or from the borrower, or both. Another technical reason not to proceed with a claim is if the grievance is already in the process of being addressed by other complainants with the same or similar grievances. In the latter case, however, the IAMs will roll subsequent complaints about the same or overlapping issues into a single complaint to better address the grievance.

Fourth, the Banks are international organisations that are owned by member states. There are instances where the Board of Directors comprised of member states has chosen not to allow a claim to proceed through the IAM, directly countering the IAM's independent recommendation. This is more pertinent to the compliance investigation phase than the problem-solving phase, because most member states view the problem-solving phase positively as a means of fixing the problem, compared with the negative fear of having an investigation made public as to the possible wrongdoings of the Banks (Park unpublished). Finally, another reason not to reject a claim for being assessed as eligible is if the financing was undertaken through financial instruments considered outside the purview of the IAM.[27] Further reasons not to proceed include that the project is subject to arbitral or judicial review; that the claim cannot be verified (finding no evidence to support the grievance); or that the claim has been deemed inactive (resulting from not being able to contact the claimant).

In the problem-solving phase, the IAMs assess the claim for its veracity and willingness of the parties to engage in problem-solving through a dialogue facilitated by the IAM. The process is either undertaken by lead problem-solving experts, or contracted mediation experts, who seek to address the grievances of claimants within the project scope. As evidenced, the willingness of the stakeholders is the overriding factor for determining whether a recourse is possible through this process. If problem-solving is successful, this will lead to an agreement among the parties. This is the third phase: facilitating settlement. This may be a long, protracted process with stakeholders identifying common ground and coming to agreement as to how to resolve concerns. This leads to a detailed agreement between the parties including how the issues are to be resolved and the role of the different stakeholders in making it a reality, and the timeline for doing so. If an agreement has been reached, then the complaint moves to the fourth and final phase: monitoring and close out. Monitoring is undertaken by the IAM to ensure the agreement has been reached and that the parties to the agreement uphold their commitments. The next section identifies the people's grievances based on the original claims made to the IAMs between 1994 and 2018.

Achieving Access to Justice in Environmental Matters

This section is concerned specifically with whether people sought to have their procedural environmental rights upheld in making claims to the IAMs. Currently, the IAMs have no capacity to determine whether people are better off after making a claim, in terms of stopping environmental and social harm and rectifying the damage (Naude Fourie 2012: 130; Bradlow and Naude Fourie 2011). Further research is necessary to ascertain whether the IAMs work for

---

[27] The latter only refers to the World Bank, which excluded the pilot approach for early solutions, and an instance of financing through a Bank Executed Trust Fund.

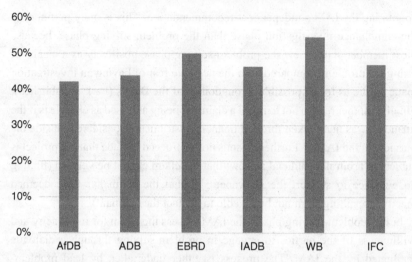

Figure 3.1 Percentage of all original submissions to the IAMs of the MDBs referencing a lack of information and/or consent, 1994–2018.

claimants as the publicly available data provided by the IAMs often does not provide this information. However, we can ascertain whether people sought to have their procedural environmental rights upheld through the process and whether they were also concerned with protecting the rights of nature beyond their own wellbeing (such as relying on the ecosystem for their livelihoods), and how they preferred to access justice for environmental matters (via problem-solving or a compliance investigation).

To identify whether claimants were seeking to have their procedural environmental rights upheld compared with the rights of nature, an analysis of all the original known claims was undertaken. These were coded according to these three categories using NVIVO12. A total of 394 complaints were coded up to the end of 2018. Significantly, owing to the confidentiality of many claims, particularly by the CAO of the World Bank Group, many of the known claim's original submissions are not publicly available. There are also claims yet to be made public by IAMs like the Inter-American Development Bank's, and some that have not yet been translated into English. Nevertheless, the results are striking with an average of 49 per cent of claims publicly available referencing a lack of information and or consent (Figure 3.1). The claims therefore reveal that half of the people making claims to the IAMs do so based on not knowing what is happening in relation to the project being undertaken.[28]

---

[28] We do not compare information and participation or grievances concerning the rights of nature because the claims often reference multiple grievances.

Claims were coded according to whether the affected parties were informed, in an accessible way, which includes culturally and in terms of language. This meant also coding based on wanting their questions answered, providing them with information when it is asked for, and in a timely manner. The lack of information pertained to claims where the parties wanted their questions answered, so they know what is to happen to them, but do not necessarily desire to intervene in the deliberative process. Claims in this category are where claimants want to know what is going to happen in relation to the project, in an accessible and timely way, so they can plan around it. Claims were also coded in this category if they referred to actions of the project sponsor acquiring consent through intimidation, deception, or withholding information. Claims may also have identified the relevant operational policies and safeguard policies their claim pertained to, usually falling under violations of 'Information Disclosure'. Claims also reference whether they had been offered informed consent. While the Banks are now converging on free, prior and informed consent, the consent of the affected parties is not a requirement that all the Banks impose. Complainants often express the lack of consent as a grievance alongside their complaints about information disclosure. For this reason, both have been included in coding for a lack of information. Of the original submissions, 25 per cent went to problem-solving with this grievance.

For example, in the 2011 claim to the European Bank for Reconstruction and Development's Independent Accountability Mechanism regarding the impact of the railway bypass in Tbilisi discussed previously, Green Alternative stated:

> People especially in the Avchala district do not know to what extent their land will be affected by the construction activities, and therefore do not know whether to expect compensation or not. ... [A]larmingly, however, the compensation process has started and some affected people in the Patara Lilo and Avchala districts have already received compensation for their land and properties, yet neither the Resettlement Action Plan for the project, nor any summary of it, is available to the affected people. We are not even certain that a final version is finished or approved.[29]

This is just one example of a claim highlighting lack of access to information for the impacts on their community from a development project.

Moreover, 54 per cent of original claims also identified a lack of access to participation (Figure 3.2). The claims were coded in terms of a desire to be involved in processes to remedy or manage the project, or create policy, or to be

---

[29] Letter from Association Green Alternative to Ms Anoush Begoyan, Project Complaint Mechanism Officer for the EBRD, Subject: Complaint on Tbilisi Railway Bypass Project (Georgia), seeking project compliance review, 28 February 2011.

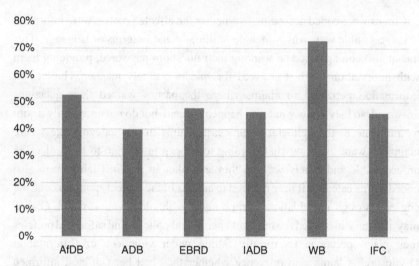

Figure 3.2 Percentage of all original submissions to the IAMs of the MDBs referencing a lack of participation, 1994–2018

included in decision-making.[30] Again, 25.6 per cent of all claims that went to problem-solving had this concern.

An example of claimants seeking to be involved in decision-making is the 2011 claim by the NGO Bridges Across Borders on behalf of 116 people being resettled for the Cambodian Rehabilitation of the Railway Project, financed by the Asian Development Bank (Request 2011/06). This is the largest relocation project in Cambodia, with thousands of people being moved to make way for the railway (Accountability Mechanism 2013: 2). Project-affected people sought compensation for resettlement, indebtedness, and a lack of access to a livelihood resulting from relocation, as well as improved basic services at the resettlement site. The claim specifically highlighted that 'before the resettlement process had begun, affected households were reporting concerns about a lack of information and consultation on the terms of the resettlement plan, as well as irregularities in the detailed measurement survey.'[31] They also noted that they had the 'right to be fully informed and closely consulted on resettlement and compensation options.'[32] The Asian Development Bank's Independent Accountability Mechanism was able to improve some complainants concerns particularly in addressing discrepancies in compensation entitlements and helping establish

---

[30] The IAMs use their own data to identify that 65 per cent of claims submitted include grievances over a lack of information, participation, and consent (Lewis 2012: 19–20)

[31] The measurement survey determined the amount of compensation according to where the inhabitants lived in relation to their distance from the railway line.

[32] Letter from Bridges across Borders Cambodia to the Special Project Facilitator, Asian Development Bank, 21 November 2011.

structures for further improvements to social services financed by Bank. The problem-solving process closed in February 2014.

Of import is how nature compares with claims made by people seeking access to justice in environmental matters for their procedural environmental rights. While many environmental concerns are also human rights concerns, such as access to clean water or to a livelihood dependent on an ecosystem, we also sought to identify whether claimants identified separate concerns regarding the right to exist, to regenerate, and to be restored when damaged. Coding therefore sought to identify the environment for the environment's sake, independent of its relationship to or impact on people. This refers to the impact that will happen to the environment, for example, the loss of biodiversity, or the loss of a species' traditional habitat, without discussion of how this impacts the complainant. This usually included words like ecosystem, flora, fauna, endangered, species, biodiversity, and ecological balance. Some complaints discuss the environment in an ambiguous way, making it difficult to know if the issue the complainant has is with the environment for its own sake, or with the human use of the environment. To be coded under this theme, it had to be a clear case of the former. In total, 27 per cent of all the original claims submitted to the IAMs reference the environment in this way; 48 per cent of all claims going to problem-solving identified environmental issues separate from claimants needs as an issue to be addressed. This indicates that people are more willing to engage in dialogue to address harms to nature than to seek recourse for a lack of enforcement of procedural environmental rights.

An example of claimants seeking recourse for the rights of nature is the 2018 claim made by eleven people of Santa Cruz de La India, Nicaragua, against the Condor gold mine being financed by the International Finance Corporation of the World Bank Group. In the claim, requestors pointed to a lack of information and a lack of consultation in relation to the project and outlined their concerns that the mine would impact the area's water quality and quantity, have potential impacts to biodiversity, increase the risk of seismic activity leading to landslides, and risk their displacement. In relation to the rights of nature, the claim stated:

> Open-pit mining would generate severe environmental impacts upon the fauna of the area and surrounding ecosystems. In particular, this area has a dry tropical forest. This ecosystem is one of the country's most threatened; mining exploitation would cause the biological connectivity between the habitats of this ecosystem to be seriously affected. Also, removing the vegetative cover would interrupt the flow of species between habitats, principally the birds and the small mammals, who depend on the habitats in order to

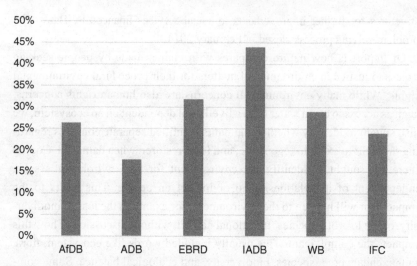

Figure 3.3 Percentage of all original submissions to the IAMs of the MDBs referencing harm to nature, 1994–2018

find water and food. This would compromise the conservation of the ecosystems of the area and of the species that depend upon these ecosystems.[33]

The claim was accepted as bona fide and was assessed for a viable problem-solving process but the requestors determined that they preferred a compliance investigation instead. Ultimately the Compliance Advisor Ombudsman determined that an investigation did not raise 'substantial concerns regarding environmental and social outcomes and/or issues of systemic importance to IFC that would warrant a compliance investigation.'[34] The case was then closed.

The data therefore makes it apparent that a lack of access to information, participation, and concern for the rights of nature are significant reasons for people to make claims to the IAMs. Although many of the concerns for recourse are for breaches of environmental procedural rights, these often occurred with concerns for the rights of nature independent of the rights of people within their environment, and other claims (such as the unequal distribution of impacts of the project on their community).[35] Therefore, the IAMs can provide not only recourse for procedural environmental rights in accordance with the protection

---

[33] Claim submitted to the Compliance Advisor Ombudsman of the World Bank Group by the Peoples of the community of La India, Santa Cruz, municipality of Santa Rosa del Penon, in the Department of Leon, Nicaragua, in relation to the project number 32519.

[34] Compliance Advisor Ombudsman, 2020, 'Case: Nicaragua / Condor Gold-01/Santa Cruz de la India'. Washington, DC, CAO. www.cao-ombudsman.org/cases/case_detail.aspx?id=1278. Accessed 10 May 2020.

[35] In terms of the frequency of concerns, unfair distributional costs are the most predominant grievance, followed by lack of participation, lack of access to information. Much further behind

standards first established by the World Bank, but for the rights of nature also. More research is still required on whether the Banks have provided effective remedy to claimants and to nature for those breaches beyond the case described previously. The next section examines what happens to claims that go to problem-solving.

Claims that Go to Problem-Solving at the IAMs

This section provides data and analysis on the claims that go to problem-solving. Relatively few claims are made to the IAMs. For all the Banks, registered claims reflect less than one per cent of their annual number of projects (Park unpublished). The number of claims is relatively low: 1,052 known claims made between 1994 with the creation of the World Bank Inspection Panel and mid 2019.[36] The IAMs are aware of the relatively small number of claims the IAMs receive. The IAMs are reviewed by their Banks every two to five years, and every review of the IAMs has made access a priority. On the one hand, this could be understood as stemming from the Banks taking their environmental and social protection standards seriously, such that there are not very many projects in the Banks' portfolios that contribute to environmental and social harm. On the other hand, it may be that there are considerable barriers to people making claims: this may come from a lack of information, or capacity, or from fear of state or corporate reprisal as noted in Section 1. Or it may stem from most requests to IAMs being routed to the operations department to have their initial concerns directed to the appropriate people. Scholars caution that the limited number of claims might not be an accurate indicator of the need for recourse (Naude Fourie 2012: 129).

Not only are the number of claims submitted to the IAMs low, but there are even fewer that meet the eligibility criteria to be registered: on average, 52 per cent of claims are registered by the IAMs. This includes whether the claim is intended for problem-solving or compliance investigation. Even when focusing on problem-solving only, the number is 45 per cent. The African, Asian, and Inter-American Development Banks are similar in the number of claims rejected for registration, while the European Bank for Reconstruction and Development has rejected 77 per cent of claims, compared with the World Bank Group which only rejected 32 per cent (see Figure 3.4). This raises questions as to the barriers to entry for registration by the European Bank for

---

is a negative impact on the environment. This is in terms of the number of claims that identify these grievances, as well as the frequency of the grievance within the claim.

[36] The database final update was 3 July 2019. This compares with only 394 publicly available original claims accessible through the IAMs online case registries, last checked December 2018.

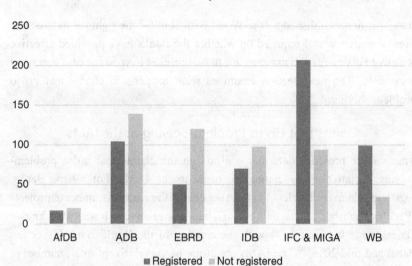

Figure 3.4 Number of complaints registered versus not registered by the IAMs of the MDBs, 1994–2019[37]

Reconstruction and Development's IAM compared with the other Banks, and the relative ease of being registered with the CAO for the World Bank Group.

The World Bank Inspection Panel has, from the beginning, been transparent in identifying all claims submitted on its online public registry, including those it did not register and why. The rest of the IAMs have become more transparent over time, by providing data on claims registered and non-registered.[38] Previously, rejected claims were discussed in annual reports but it was not clear if all requests were included and the IAMs had significant discretion as to whether they tracked all interactions with people or only documented a full claim assessable for registration (see Park 2015, for example). The World Bank and the World Bank Group have the highest rates of receiving and registering claims, which befits their global reach (see Figure 3.4). Many of the non-registered claims are so because they do not meet the aforementioned criteria in terms of not being about a project financed by the Banks, not linked to the Banks actions or inactions, not related to environmental and social harm, or not having first gone to the Bank's operations to discuss the grievance. There is no clear trend as to specific causes for not registering claims (Park 2019).

As mentioned in the previous section, NGOs have identified that the IAMs accepted half of the claims submitted to them and only twenty per cent lead to a successful mediation or a compliance investigation report being undertaken

---

[37] This includes complaints going to a compliance investigation.
[38] See the individual websites of the IAMs of the MDBs.

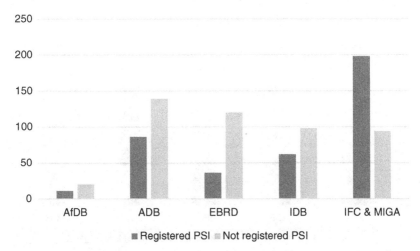

Figure 3.5 Number of complaints registered versus not registered by the IAMs of the MDBs for problem-solving initiatives, 1994–2019

(Huijstee et al. 2016). Data on the IAMs from Park (2019) confirms that nearly half of the claims submitted are registered as bona fide claims for problem-solving (45 per cent), and half of those registered are deemed eligible for problem-solving (see Figures 3.3, 3.4, and 3.5). Of those registered that enter the problem-solving phase, 40.8 per cent move into the facilitating and settlement phase, with 18.2 per cent of those leading to an agreement with monitoring towards closing the complaint. This is similar to Huijstee et al.'s findings (2016).

What this means is that only approximately one quarter of all claims submitted to the IAMs are eligible for problem-solving, with only 10.5 per cent of all claims submitted moving into the facilitating and settlement phase, and only 2.7 per cent of all claims submitted leading to an agreement with monitoring towards closing the complaint. However, we cannot take the number of claims submitted as the baseline, because they do not accurately reflect the fact that the registration process is a means of identifying bona fide grievances for which access to justice in environmental matters is available. Although we have identified the narrow parameters of the process for justice in environmental matters, the registration criteria do allow for recourse for environmental and social harm. Indeed, claims are rejected by the IAMs for a variety of valid reasons, with no clear evidence that assessing claims for access is unjust (Park 2019).

Nevertheless, there is a significant drop in the number of claims at each stage of the process (Figure 3.5). However, the figures do not consider that there are ongoing claims at each stage. In other words, it is not that there is a drop of

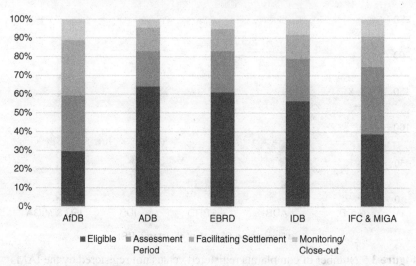

Figure 3.6 Results of claims going to the problem-solving initiative for the IAMs of the MDBs, 1994–2019

12.2 per cent between the 53 per cent of claims accepted problem-solving in the assessment phase (to determine whether problem-solving can help address claimants grievances as denoted in Figure 3.3) to the 40.8 per cent that move into the facilitating and settlement phase, because this does not take into account the ongoing nature of a number of claims in the assessment phase. The data can only provide a snapshot of where claims are at any one stage of the problem-solving process. It can identify claims that have moved onto another stage, or at what stage claims have run their course, but these figures do not consider ongoing negotiations. In other words, currently 40.8 per cent of claims have moved into the facilitating a settlement phase but this is not a final figure. The same goes for claims that have made it to the monitoring and close-out phase, of which there are currently 18.2 per cent. Figure 3.6, therefore, provides a current snapshot of how many claims have made it to each stage in the problem-solving process.

There is significant variation across the Banks in terms of how many claims go through problem-solving and their outcomes. By numbers, the Asian Development Bank and the European Bank for Reconstruction and Development look poor in terms of the relatively few claims that make it to the successful monitoring of an agreement and closing of the complaint (7 per cent and 8 per cent), with the Inter-American Development Bank at 15 per cent, and the World Bank Group at 23 per cent. The African Development Bank has the most 'successful' record with 38 per cent, but it also has the smallest number of complaints overall (see Figure 3.3; for more on the variation among the Banks see Park unpublished).

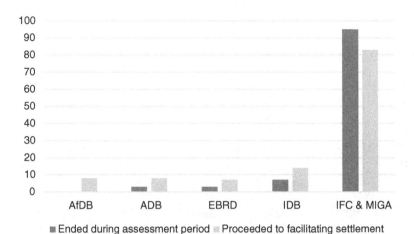

Figure 3.7 Number of complaints which proceeded versus did not proceed past assessment at the IAMs of the MDBs for problem-solving initiatives, 1994–2019

Once registered, on average 53 per cent of claims for problem-solving move into the assessment phase. There is again middle ground with the Asian and Inter-American Development Banks and the European Bank for Reconstruction and Development having similar rates of claims where problem-solving is undertaken. The African Development Bank has 100 per cent rate of claims able to engage in problem-solving, while the World Bank Group's rate is 47 per cent (see Figure 3.7).

Once identified as viable for problem-solving, the main concern is why problem-solving does not proceed. While there are instances of all of the reasons for problem-solving to fail as listed earlier, overwhelmingly, the basis for not being able to undertake, or fail while attempting to undertake, problem-solving is because the parties cannot agree to do so.[39] For example, for the World Bank Group, 67 per cent of problem-solving fails because either the claimant (19 per cent), or the borrower (38 per cent), or both (10 per cent) no longer want to engage. For the Inter-American Development Bank, it is 55 per cent: 33 per cent of claimants, compared with 11 per cent of borrowers, and another 11 per cent where both do not want to proceed. Another 22 per cent of claims do not proceed to problem-solving at the Inter-American Development Bank because they are under judicial review, which may or may not affect the claim.

For example, in 2010, a local committee was established called the SIEPAC– La Alfombra Committee on behalf of the La Alfombra Community in Costa

---

[39] All data is taken from Park 2019.

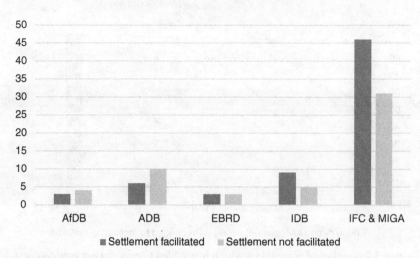

Figure 3.8 Number of complaints where a settlement has been facilitated compared with claims where settlement not possible through IAM problem-solving, 1994–2019

Rica, to challenge an Inter-American Development Bank–funded project, the Electric Interconnection System for the Central American Countries (SIEPAC). The claim alleged that part of an electricity transmission line running through the community could have significant environmental and social impacts including affecting the amount and quality of water and impacts on the fragile soil in the area: it would run across the Paso de la Danta Biological Corridor thus fragmenting habitat for local species, and affect local ecotourism. An eligibility assessment for problem-solving was undertaken but the differences between the stakeholders was too great for conciliation to take place. The case then went to the compliance investigation function of the Inter-American Development Bank's IAM but it was then discovered that a local company had instigated two claims in the Costa Rican Environmental Administrative Court against the project (ICIM 2011b). The claim was therefore deemed ineligible for a compliance investigation and the case was closed. The inadmissibility of a claim seeking access to justice for environmental matters because the project is subject to judicial review has been identified by the Inter-American Development Bank itself as preventing access to justice (IDB 2012b: 19–20).

For the Asian Development Bank, 25 per cent of claims do not proceed because claimants no longer want to continue with the process, indicating a problem with using problem-solving to address people's grievances. Another 50 per cent of claims do not proceed because the Asian Development Bank states that actions are already underway to address claimants' concerns,

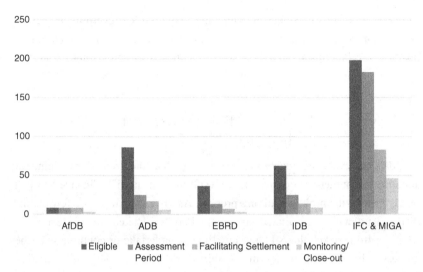

Figure 3.9 Stages of the problem-solving initiative by IAM of the MDBs, 1994–2019

where the IAM has allowed Bank management discretion for addressing grievances that may prevent access to justice in environmental matters (Park 2015). The remaining 25 per cent do not continue because the Bank is no longer financing the project. The European Bank for Reconstruction and Development is unique in that all 100 per cent of its problem-solving has not progressed because the Bank is either not, not yet, or no longer financing the project. This means that claimants might be pre-emptively making claims against projects likely to be funded by the EBRD and where a problem-solving initiative is not viable, or where the project sponsor has decided not to proceed with financing from the Bank (which may or may not result from the lodging of a claim with the Bank's IAM). In comparison, the African Development Bank has accepted all its claims for problem-solving (of eight submissions), generally using this as a first step in the process for access to justice in environmental matters.

Overall, 56 per cent of claims that make it to the facilitating settlement phase have ended with an agreement of the parties. This ranges from the lowest with the Asian Development Bank having 38 per cent end with an agreement to the highest with the World Bank Group at 60 per cent. This indicates how difficult it is to achieve access to justice through problem-solving. Even at this stage, relations among the parties may break down and the process may fail. The problem-solving process is often lengthy, requiring ongoing commitment of all the parties. Changes to the interests and preferences of the parties may change, as may the players in the process. For example, corporations may be bought, sold, or merged, equity stakes in companies may be sold, governments may be swept from office, and community leaders may change or may change their position in relation to the issues at stake. The next section examines what this means for achieving access to justice in environmental matters.

Evaluating Access to Justice in Environmental Matters through Problem-Solving

The data provided previously demonstrates a clear picture of how claims to address environmental and social harm resulting from an MDB financed project move through the problem-solving process. As discussed, there are few claims that end up with a facilitated settlement between stakeholders, most often resulting from stakeholders being unwilling to undertake or continue with the process. This section locates this within broader experiences of mediation before examining whether claimants' environmental procedural rights, and the rights of nature, are being addressed through problem-solving.

One of the most significant issues in seeking to evaluate the IAMs in undertaking problem-solving, is how to do so. Problem-solving, like Ombudsman offices and broader alternative dispute resolution processes, are difficult to evaluate in terms of their effectiveness. Although Section 2 identified how IGMs should operate based on their own understandings of their activities and how they are reviewed by the UN, the broader Ombudsman and alternative dispute resolution literature has also grappled with how to evaluate effectiveness based on process and outcomes. These are worth reviewing considering questions as to whether the data provided demonstrates difficulty accessing justice including how it is being administered. Evaluating effectiveness may be based on five factors: claim outcomes, the number of complaints, benchmarking, self-evaluation, and cost (Stuhmcke 2018).

First, the basis for evaluating problem-solving effectiveness cannot be purely on whether complainants get what they want. While it is important that people's concerns are heard, an evaluation of the process must identify whether it has done what it sought to do. In Ombuds offices, this is to remove the maladministration in public administration, initially by the state but increasingly by the corporate sector and now by international organisations. Fundamental to the conception of the Ombuds role is that it was designed, in its modern equivalent, as a non-judicial alternative for overseeing public administration. It was a domestic institution established to protect individual rights and democracy through upholding the rule of law against maladministration through soft powers of investigation, recommendations, and reporting (Carl 2018: 20). Problem-solving seeks to address environmental and social grievances where harm has resulted from the acts or omissions of the Banks in following their protection standards. The aim therefore is not to necessarily give claimants what they want, but to provide recourse where the Banks have failed to uphold their protection standards. Clearly the IAM should, where able, provide the means for redressing valid grievances although they have no remit for collecting or assessing if people are satisfied with the process.

The difficulty with the IAMs, as noted earlier, is that they depend on whether the grievance fits within the project agreed to by the Bank and the project sponsor. Thus, the process prescribes access to some forms of justice in environmental matters. As noted, there is variation across the Banks suggesting where individual Banks may fall short of providing access to justice in environmental matters in specific phases of the problem-solving process, for example, through barriers to entry, discretion as to whether to accept the claim, and being able to facilitate problem-solving that takes into account the concerns of the claimants. However, the generally smaller number of agreements reached between the parties may not be indicative of a failure of process, where efforts to provide recourse to address grievances have been just.

Even if the process is just, this may not necessarily lead to better community outcomes overall. For example, large-scale projects like the Cambodian Railway may have widespread adverse impacts affecting large populations but only those who formally complain may have their problems addressed (Connell 2015). This means that there may be an increase in community tension between those whose harm is addressed compared with those whose harm is not. This may be exacerbated by the support provided by local, national, and international NGOs supporting claimants in opposition to the development project (Ziai 2016).

Second, Ombuds and alternative dispute resolution processes often attempt to determine whether the office, through its actions and advice, plays a role in stemming further complaints. All the offices have information powers in terms of identifying peoples' rights in areas of their competence. However, it is quite difficult to causally determine the role an IAM or ombuds office plays in affecting the number of complaints they receive. There is no evidence that the IAMs, through their actions, have contributed to a reduction in the number of claims they receive, although one avenue of research does seek to determine what may influence the submission of a claim (Hunter 2003). When the IAMs were originally conceived, the Banks were worried that any advertising the IAMs did to make known their existence would 'drum up business' (Park unpublished), although the low registration rates have shown this not to be a problem. Thus, the problem remains that high numbers of complaints may indicate injustice, but low complaint rates do not necessarily equate with either just administration or the meeting of environmental and social protection standards (Stuhmcke n.d).

Third, benchmarking is often undertaken as a means of evaluating effectiveness either through whether the office is meeting its evaluation criteria (as outlined in Section 2) or in meeting the same outputs as the other IAMs. All the IAMs tend to benchmark against one another in terms of their processes and standards, and these are re-examined by their Banks in periodic reviews over time. This, in turn, has led to a convergence of their practices (Park unpublished). It is not clear if the IAMs are concerned with how they benchmark against one another in terms of the outcomes of their complaints. This may stem from significant variation in terms of their volume. However, outside the African Development Bank's IAM, they tend to demonstrate similar trends in outcomes (see Figure 3.6), which may indicate that the Banks are undertaking similar approaches to enacting access to justice in environmental matters, although the Compliance Advisor Ombudsman has a higher rate of accepting claims for assessment and therefore for facilitating a settlement.[40]

Fourth, analysis of Ombuds or alternative dispute resolution office effectiveness is often undertaken by the offices themselves. Given that only the office itself tends to have up-to-date and accurate data, especially in relation to confidential claims, they are the only ones with the ability to truly assess their performance (see, for example, Lewis 2012, which uses the data from the offices themselves). However, it is often difficult to generalise from the idiosyncrasies of each office, with a proliferation and permutation of practices under this moniker (Hertogh and Kirkham 2018). Studies identify a range of resolution of cases, from 35 per cent for corporate Ombuds offices to 97 per cent for some state Ombudsman (Harrison 2004: 315). Some also look at client satisfaction with the process, which the IAMs do not do. Although each IAM provides an annual report of their activities, it is the review undertaken by the Banks themselves which tends to evaluate their practices and their effectiveness. The Banks and their shareholders tend to have different interests than the IAMs in terms of what they hope to achieve. This is important because the reviews of the IAMs also tend not to look to the outcome of the problem-solving process as an indicator of success. The review process is often where the interests of the IAMs come up against the shareholders, with input from civil society including NGOs and accountability consultants.

This leads to the next point, which is concern for cost. The Banks and their shareholders are not only concerned with whether the IAMs can address

---

[40] The outlier here is the AfDB where there are very few claims and no up-to-date data on their outcomes. Nevertheless, of the known outcomes, the AfDB has been successful in addressing complainants concerns through problem-solving.

grievances, but also how long it takes and the cost of doing so. This fits with broader general Ombuds and alternative dispute resolution offices that are concerned with the effective use of resources. This is often evaluated in terms of the costs of maintaining an office as well as the cost to the organisation for the time spent by staff in responding to claimants (Stuhmcke n.d). Although the Banks query the costs of responding to claimants' concerns, problem-solving is not a quick or easy solution. However, given that it is a last resort, it is often the only response left. It also can lead to sustainable development where before, without access to justice in environmental matters, there may not have been. Moreover, concern for costs for addressing grievances is not built into the costs of project delivery. In other words, the presumption is that this is an additional cost to be passed on to the borrower rather than factoring in whether high risk or high environmental impact projects are likely to cause grievance that will need to be addressed if the protection standards are not adhered to. This is particularly important given claimants' demands for having their procedural environmental rights recognised, which is detailed in Section 4 on compliance investigations.

Conclusion

The section has identified that claimants are seeking recourse for a lack of access to information, and a lack of access to participation through the IAMs and through the problem-solving process. They are also seeking recourse for harm or violations to the rights of nature independent of human concerns. Yet problem-solving can only work if it is in the interests of claimants, the Bank, the government, and/or the project sponsor (for non-sovereign loans). This section identified the limitations of what the IAMs can provide access to justice in environmental matters for, and if affected people's concerns can be integrated into the project. It laid out how the IAM problem-solving process works and how claims move through the stages. IAMs have some discretion, which needs thorough investigation to determine if they are just. There is also some variability between the Banks' IAMs, also requiring further examination. Overall, however, it is difficult to determine how to evaluate the outcome of a request for problem-solving given the IAM's constraints, and the means of evaluating them. As noted herein, this is complicated by the fact that most of the information is known only by the IAMs, that shareholders and the Banks tend to evaluate them differently, and that process rather than outcome matters for whether justice has been served. Section 4 looks at whether claimants seeking a compliance investigation have their concerns addressed regarding a lack of access to information, a lack of access to participation, and concerns of the rights of nature.

4 Access to Justice in Environmental Matters through the Compliance Investigations of the Independent Accountability Mechanisms of the MDBs

This section examines whether compliance investigations provide access to justice in environmental matters. Like Section 3, it analyses the process of triggering investigation based on a claim submitted to the IAM, specifying whether claimants want problem-solving or a compliance investigation. The first section documents how claims move through the process to determine whether a claim meets the criteria for an investigation, how an investigation is undertaken, and what happens once an investigation is complete. Second, we detail what the data looks like on claims that go to compliance investigation, in terms of claimants seeking recourse for procedural environmental rights and the rights of nature. We then review whether the Banks have been found in non-compliance in relation to these rights, which allows the IAMs the ability to monitor to bring the Bank back into compliance with environmental and social standards.

What Is a Compliance Investigation?

Compliance investigations remain the tool favoured by NGOs and states to force companies and international organisations to follow environmental and social regulations. This section analyses the process for addressing grievances through compliance investigations. This includes how they are assessed as eligible for investigation, how an investigation is undertaken, and how deliberations for findings of non-compliance are made, including how the Banks' boards and management respond. It is worth reiterating that remedies such as stopping the harm and rectifying damage remain with Bank management. Management is in turn, directed by how the Banks' shareholders (member states) respond to findings of non-compliance by the IAMs. This means that the compliance investigation tool is considered a hard stick to force the Banks to rectify problems caused by the Banks' acts or omissions in relation to environmental and social standards, but there are many links in the chain between a complaint seeking recourse and the final outcome.

As with the problem-solving process, a claim must first be registered according to the criteria outlined in Section 4. The Banks differ in terms of how claims are accepted for compliance investigation. For example, up until September 2020, the World Bank's Inspection Panel only undertakes compliance but the Compliance Advisor Ombudsman from 1999, and the Asian and Inter-American Development Bank's from 2012 and 2010, respectively, all had bifurcated sequential processes that required claimants to go through problem-solving even if this is not what they wanted. This frequently delayed identifying and rectifying Bank non-compliance causing harm. For the African Development Bank and the European Bank for Reconstruction and Development, claimants could choose mediation or compliance review or both could be undertaken simultaneously. Unless claimants clearly state their preferences from the beginning, the mechanisms tended to review the process through problem-solving first, before determining whether a compliance review would be applicable. In the 2000s, the IAMs shifted to allow claimants to determine if they prefer problem-solving or compliance investigation.[41]

A compliance investigation can only be triggered if claimants believe that it leads to harm or the threat of harm; and harm can only be addressed if it results from a policy violation (Clark et al. 2003: 267; Lewis 2012: 26). Again, this is based on two or more people in the project site or affected area or their representative, such as a lawyer or NGO, although the European Bank for Reconstruction and Development now allows NGOs to make claims independent of people directly affected by the project. The Compliance Advisor Ombudsman of the World Bank Group differs from the other IAMs in relation to compliance investigations because it can trigger investigations via different pathways. It can do so as a result of claims from people seeking recourse for harm but it also has three other triggers: first, it has 'own motion' powers where the CAO Ombudsman can trigger an investigation as noted in Section 1; second, the World Bank Group President also has the capacity to trigger a compliance investigation, which has occurred in the past; and third, unsuccessful problem-solving initiatives now automatically trigger a compliance investigation to determine the cause of the harm.

For example, in 2005, the World Bank Group President Paul Wolfowitz triggered a compliance investigation over claims of human rights abuses at the Dikilushi Copper-Silver Mine in the Democratic Republic of Congo, after reports in international media of such allegations. The Multilateral Investment Guarantee Agency of the World Bank Group provided a political risk guarantee for the Anvil Mine. The Compliance Advisor Ombudsman found that MIGA had 'weaknesses in following' due diligence in relation to its environmental and social review procedures (ESRPs) and 'on conflict and security issues specifically, [which] echo a number of concerns they had already raised' in reviewing MIGA's environmental and social policies (CAO 2006: 8). The CAO kept the compliance audit open until the World Bank Group had addressed the non-compliance.

---

[41] If claimants chose problem-solving then they could still go to the compliance investigation function but if they chose a compliance investigation this generally precluded going to problem-solving afterwards.

One of the striking aspects of the compliance investigation process as it was originally constructed was the limited role in the process for complainants. Once they submitted the claim, complainants would then wait to be informed as to whether it had been accepted as eligible for investigation. They might then be contacted to provide evidence during the investigation. As the first of the IAMs, the World Bank Inspection Panel established as its own rules of procedure that claimants should be informed directly as to the outcome of the investigation as this was not detailed in the resolution creating it (Inspection Panel 2009: xi). Claimants are increasingly being invited to comment on the IAM's findings and Bank management's response (for the World Bank, Asian Development Bank, and the European Bank for Reconstruction and Development), but complainants do not have a formal role in developing remedial action plans to rectify damage (Naude Fourie 2012: 125–6).

Once a claim has been submitted and registered (see Section 3), the claim is then assessed to determine whether it is eligible for investigation. The criteria for eligibility, like with the problem-solving initiative, are as follows:

- there is reason to believe that the harm is being caused by the project because of Bank's acts or omissions;
- there are not already actions underway by Bank management to address claimants' grievances;
- the claim raises substantial concerns regarding environmental and social outcomes that would warrant an investigation;
- the grievance is still a concern and can be verified;
- the Board has approved the recommendation for an investigation;
- there is no judicial review of the project.

Compliance investigations can hold the Banks accountable for past or existing action with an indirect aim of preventing future wrongdoing through documenting findings of the non-compliance. If the aim is to provide a formal sanctioning process for evaluating whether the Bank's acts or omissions have led to harm, and then establishing sanctions to prevent reoccurrences, then the original design of the mechanisms left much to be desired. The earlier versions of the mechanisms did not include functions that would enable the IAMs to provide recommendations on how to address claimants' concerns and become policy compliant, or the capacity to monitor the Bank's responses to findings of non-compliance. For example, the Inspection Panel does not produce recommendations but rather reports its findings to the Board, although these have been written in such a way as to suggest recommendations as to how to remedy the problem (Inspection Panel 2009: 41). How to respond to the IAM reports were left to the board and to Bank management, making it difficult to ensure remedy for people affected by MDB-financed projects. This has also changed over time with all the IAMs, bar the Inspection Panel, now being able to make recommendations on how to provide redress for the damage or to bring the project into compliance.

Based on the eligibility of the claim and a preliminary review of the material, a decision is made by the IAM whether or not to recommend an investigation either to the Bank's board or to the president, with different IAMs coming under either Bank management or the Bank's board. For example, the European Bank for Reconstruction and Development and the World Bank Group's IAMs report to the president, while the Inspection Panel, the Inter-American and Asian Development Bank's later IAM iterations report to their boards. Over time, the IAMs have become more independent of their Banks, with most now providing recommendations to their presidents or boards that are accepted on a 'no objection' basis.[42] This has been a long process, with advocates arguing that IAMs should be fully independent from the Banks in making decisions to investigate based on the impartiality and credibility of their office as per the evaluation criteria discussion in Section 2. Bank management have also sought and won the right to counter the grievances presented by claimants. Once a claim is registered, Bank management has a right of reply, which informs the IAM as to whether a claim is eligible for investigation. Based on this evidence, the IAM then determines whether a claim should be investigated. One of the reasons not to investigate is whether the IAM is assured that Bank management is already addressing the problem. Again, specific investigation not only into each of the Banks but also the claims is necessary to determine whether the Banks act justly in their deliberations.

An investigation comprises gathering evidence, including desk reviews of the Bank's activities; accessing and compiling documents; undertaking interviews with claimants, Bank staff, and specialists; and field site visits. This recreates the decision-making process by the Banks' operation teams, which led to management approving the project. Generally, site visits by the IAMs are accepted by the Banks' borrowers except in the Asian Development Bank where this was considered a violation of state sovereignty. This has led to two stand-offs between the IAM and the borrower regarding projects in Thailand

---

[42] Although there are three cases at the Inter-American Development Bank where the Board has rejected the recommendations for investigation by its IAM: the Santa Barbara-Rurrenabaque Northern Corridor Highway Improvement Program claim (MICI-BO-2011–013); the Mario Covas Rodoanel Project – Northern Section 1 and Mário Covas Rodoanel – Northern Sections 1 and 2 (MICI-BR-2011–015 and MICI-BR-2011–022).

and China.[43] Given the strength of protecting state sovereignty as a norm in the region, the Asian Development Bank's IAM continues to rely on the willingness of borrower member states and the good offices of Bank management to allow the IAM to conduct site visits and thoroughly investigate independently of interference or constraint (Park 2015).

The process of investigation is highly contentious, with staff across the Banks often feeling like they are being interrogated, while the Bank's calculate the costs of amassing information required for the investigations to be conducted. Practices also vary in terms of how willing Bank staff and management are in cooperating with an investigation. The highly technical nature of some of the claims regarding the environmental and social harms means that the IAMs often must employ scientists to conduct the investigations in addition to their panellists (such as hydrologists in relation to dams, or anthropologists in relation to Indigenous Peoples). The IAMs vary from having panel members for fixed terms, such as five years like the Inspection Panel and the Asian Development Bank's Independent Accountability Mechanism, compared with having a roster of experts on retainer that are employed based on the claims coming forward like the African and Inter-American Development Banks and the European Bank for Reconstruction and Development. Owing to the confrontational process for creating the World Bank Inspection Panels, there remains a highly legalistic framing of Inspection Panel investigations, with Bank management countering nearly all claims of breaches of standards leading to harm. This means that both 'sides' have their technical experts to refute the other.

Once an investigation has been conducted, the IAM then presents its findings and/or recommendations to the Bank. Previously, this meant that the IAM's job was done, and the response to the findings and recommendations were the purview of the Banks' boards or management. This remains the case with the Inspection Panel, although in 67 per cent of all cases of non-compliance the Bank's board has asked the panel to monitor Bank management in implementing management action plans to bring the project into compliance (Park 2019). However, starting with the CAO of the World Bank Group, the IAMs began to acquire monitoring provisions that would enable them to assess whether Bank management was responding to, and implementing, their recommendations. Nearly all the mechanisms now have monitoring powers over Bank actions after an investigation has revealed non-compliance. Monitoring is increasingly seen as useful by member states as an effective sanctioning tool for holding the

---

[43] Regarding the Samut Prakan Waste Water Project in Thailand (Loan number 1410-THA) and the Fuzhou Environmental Improvement Project in China (Loan number 2176-PRC).

Banks to account, forcing them to become policy compliant at the project level. Banks then must provide the IAM with their management action plan, which details what they have done and plan to do to rectify the problem. Depending on the Bank, the IAM then continues to assess whether the Banks have become compliant in addressing the problem or whether more monitoring is required. Some, like the European Bank for Reconstruction and Development, require monitoring reports every six months. The Asian Development Bank did enable its independent accountability mechanism to monitor the Bank's compliance for five years from 2003, but then limited it to two years in its most recent review (ADB 2012).

Some of the mechanisms are also allowed to provide their Banks with advice and lessons learned from their experience with complaints. For example, the CAO has robust advisory powers but the IAMs for the Asian, African (from 2015), and Inter-American Development Banks (from 2014) can provide lessons learned. The World Bank's Inspection Panel does not have specific provisions to provide advice although it does produce publications discussing general trends and systemic issues. The European Bank for Reconstruction and Development's mechanism is mandated to feed the results of its findings into the review of the Bank's environmental and social policies, providing robust provisions for improving the standards considering Bank operations (EBRD 2014). This is important because the mechanisms can then meet the UN Guiding Principles for IGM's to improve continuous learning.

Achieving Access to Justice in Environmental Matters

This section is concerned specifically with whether people sought to have their procedural environmental rights upheld in requesting a compliance investigation (or having one triggered for them). Again, referring to the 394 original claims compiled from the publicly available submissions to the IAMs between 1994 and the end of 2018 (Figure 3.7), we know that 49 per cent of claims submitted reference a lack of information and or consent. In terms of the original complaints identifying a lack of information as a grievance, of those, 139 went to either straight compliance investigation or both (35 per cent), while 155 cited an absence of participation in either straight compliance investigation, or in claims that went to both problem-solving and a compliance investigation (39 per cent). As mentioned in Section 3, 27 per cent of all the 394 original claims submitted to the IAMs reference the environment as separate from people's dependence on it and 84 (21 per cent) of those went either straight to compliance investigation or a combination of problem-solving and investigation. Notably, claims that reference a lack of information, participation, and harm to nature independent of the claimant's reliance on it, are more likely to go to compliance than problem-solving alone. This might speak to the claimant's awareness of the breaches of the Banks' policies triggering demand for a compliance investigation. It also speaks to claimants' desire for independent evaluation of the harm being done to nature.

A lack of access to information, participation, and concern for the rights of nature are significant reasons for people to make claims to the IAMs. Frequently, the grievances reference breaches of environmental procedural rights alongside concerns for the rights of nature independent of the rights of people. Therefore, the IAMs can provide not only recourse for procedural environmental rights in accordance with the protection standards first established by the World Bank, but also for the rights of nature. Although more research is still required on whether the Banks have provided effective remedy to claimants and to nature for those breaches, the following outlines the findings of the compliance investigations.

Seeking Recourse through Compliance Investigations

This section documents the claims that have gone to compliance as a means of access to justice in environmental matters, with reference to whether the claims reference procedural environmental rights (access to information and participation). It details whether compliance investigations reveal non-compliance, and how the Banks have responded. Despite providing evidence of harm resulting from Bank non-compliance with its own protection standards, compliance investigations also may be of limited use for addressing breaches of procedural environmental rights given that the projects continue to be built while the investigation is underway.

As with the problem-solving initiative process, we cannot start from the number of claims that have been registered because of the lack of complete information on claims that have rejected over time, although 52 per cent of all known claims are registered as bona fide. Once registered, many claims went through the problem-solving process, so by the time they went to compliance investigation they were already deemed eligible according to the criteria for problem-solving. If claimants then decided that they wanted a compliance investigation to be undertaken, the claim was then appraised to determine its eligibility for an investigation based on the criteria detailed earlier in the section.

On average, 47 per cent of claims that go to the compliance function are recommended for an investigation during the appraisal stage, compared with

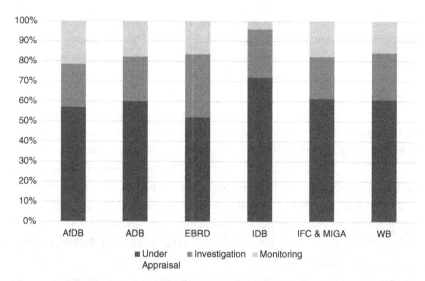

Figure 4.1 Outcomes of the claims proceeding to compliance investigation by the IAMs of the MDBs, 1994–2019

65 per cent of claims that are deemed eligible for problem-solving. In some respects, comparing the problem-solving and compliance investigation processes might not be meaningful given that the aim of problem-solving is to provide recourse through engagement between the parties to resolve the grievance, compared with an investigation into wrongdoing that may or may not lead to redress. On the other hand, some communities seek both (and were compelled to undertake problem-solving first). Few claimants make it known that they are dissatisfied with the outcome of the problem-solving leading to a request for a compliance investigation (although there is evidence of dissatisfaction with the process with the Asian Development Bank; see Park 2015). Again, the Banks display slight variation with the Inter-American Development Bank as the outlier in the compliance process, with the highest requests for investigation and the fewest of the claims being found non-compliant and going to monitoring (see Figure 4.1). This has been attributed to the role of executive directors influencing the process (Park unpublished).[44]

Of the 308 claims that have gone to the compliance investigation function, 145 were recommended for an investigation (53 per cent), although only 122 were conducted (39 per cent). This includes cases where recommendations for investigations were rejected by the Banks' Boards such as early in the history of the Inspection Panel and the Asian Development Bank as well as more recent

---

[44] See the Board's responses to MICI findings in these three cases: Program to Improve Highway Corridors in Paraguay claim (MICI-PR-2010–008); Panama Canal Expansion Program claim (MICI-PN-2011–031); and the Panamanian Pando Monte-Lirio Hydroelectric Project (MICI-PN-2010–002).

cases for rejecting the findings of compliance investigations by the Inter-American Development Bank's IAM (Park 2019). Data on claims going to compliance investigation demonstrates that there is a decline in the number of cases as they progress through the process, but that this is not higher than for problem-solving (see Figure 4.1).

An example of an IAM's compliance investigation finding being rejected by the Inter-American Development Bank's board is in relation to Paraguay's road project (Program to Improve Highway Corridors in Paraguay MICI-PR-2010–008). The Compliance Review Panel stated the Inter-American Development Bank had contributed to harm of the Indigenous Ache people in not complying with its Environment Policy. The Bank's board rejected the findings, stating that the 'panel report does not provide compelling findings that would serve as evidence of Management's non-compliance.' The board went further to argue that there were 'doubts about the usefulness of the report' and that the investigation should never have been undertaken because there was an administrative error in the loan disbursement date (the loan was considered 98 per cent disbursed when the claim was lodged).[45] Thus the board rejected the findings of non-compliance, thus obviating the need to correct the damage wrought by the project.

A more detailed picture can be seen through the process by breaking it down by Bank (see Figure 4.2). Here again you can see a higher volume of complaints going to the World Bank and the World Bank Group as befits their global reach. The African Development Bank has the smallest number of complaints, but both the African Development Bank (63 per cent) and the European Bank for Reconstruction and Development (74 per cent) accept a larger number of complaints for investigation than reject them at the appraisal stage, which is what the other Banks do. The few claims that have proceeded to compliance investigation at the African Development Bank have been large-scale projects with significant environmental impacts, such as the 2007 claim for the Bujagali Hydropower Project and Bujagali Interconnection Project in Uganda, and the 2010 claim for the Medupi Power Project in South Africa (Park 2019). These demonstrate that the compliance investigation is providing access to justice in environmental matters for these claimants. Data on the European Bank for Reconstruction and Development's IAM suggests that it is a compliance-driven mechanism compared with problem-solving and does seek to hold the Bank to account for its operations (Park 2019). There is a mixed trend here with the remaining Banks

---

[45] Victoria Márquez-Mees, ICIM Executive Secretary, 12 July 2013, *PR-MICI002-2010 'Program to Improve Highway Corridors in Paraguay' (Loan 933 A/OC-PR): Final decision by the Board of Executive Directors regarding the Compliance Review Report for case PR-MICI002-2010*, ICIM, Washington, DC. Accessed 17 August 2016. http://idbdocs.iadb.org/wsdocs/getdocument .aspx?docnum=37893902

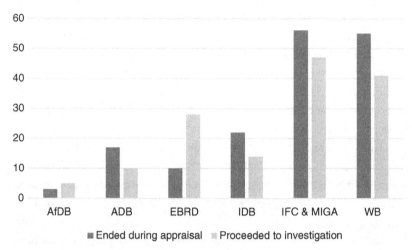

Figure 4.2 Number of claims requesting a compliance investigation that are recommended for an investigation during the appraisal stage, 1994–2019

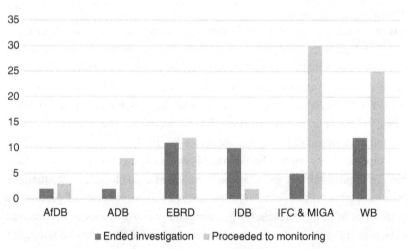

Figure 4.3 Complaints submitted to the IAMs of the MDBs found non-compliant leading to monitoring, 1994–2019.

having fewer claims go to investigation, with the Asian and Inter-American Development Bank accepting fewer (37 and 39 per cent respectively), with questions as to the role of the Bank's boards in seeking to prevent claims going to investigation, especially in the IAM's initial form (Park 2015).

On average, of the 39 per cent that were investigated, 66 per cent were found to be non-compliant and required monitoring. That means that a quarter of all claims requesting an investigation of environmental and social harms were found to have been the result of the Banks not following their own environmental and social protection standards.

Although the trend generally across the Banks is that fewer of the claims that go to appraisal are recommended for investigation (bar the African Development Bank and the European Bank for Reconstruction and Development), if a compliance investigation is undertaken and non-compliance is found, then the case requires monitoring to ensure that the Bank does become policy compliant or the grievance is adequately addressed (where possible, as outlined in Sections 2 and 3). The data reveals that the Banks generally tend to bunch together (between 29–38 per cent) in terms of the investigations leading to findings of non-compliance leading to monitoring. The World Bank Group has the lowest number of investigated projects being found non-compliant and requiring monitoring (29 per cent), compared with the highest of the African Development Bank (38 per cent). The outlier that bucks this trend is the Inter-American Development Bank with only six per cent of investigations being found non-compliant and requiring monitoring, for the reasons suggested earlier.

What protection standards are the Banks non-compliant with? There are three policies which with the Banks are predominantly found non-compliant requiring the Banks to address the grievance and seek to become policy compliant. These are general umbrella policies on environmental and social assessment (EA), the Indigenous Peoples policy, and the Disclosure of Information policy.[46] This upholds the argument that claimants are seeking to have their procedural environmental rights upheld (see Figure 4.4).

Overwhelmingly, all the Banks have been found non-compliant with their own environmental and social assessment and at a much higher rate than for other policy breaches,[47] although this varies by Bank in terms of percentage of all types of policy breaches. This umbrella policy includes environmental protection standards as well as procedural environmental rights pertaining to social impact assessments requiring information and consultation. The second

---

[46] In the read me file of the database (Park 2019) and Figure 4.4, the Bank's policies are categorised as follow: the umbrella environmental and social assessment policies are category A, B is Involuntary Settlement, C is Indigenous Peoples, D is Gender and Development, E is Physical Cultural Resources such as heritage sites, F is Natural Habitats, G is Water Resource Management, H is Poverty Reduction, I is Disclosure of Information, J is Energy, K is Resource Efficiency and Pollution Prevention, L is Labour Standards, M is Community Health, Safety, and Security, N is Disaster Risk Management, O is Operational Procedural Violations, P is where the project has been found to be compliant, and Q is where the IAM has not made explicit if the project is or is not compliant with its environmental and social policies.
[47] Although the World Bank was found equally non-compliant with its Involuntary Resettlement policy (Park 2019).

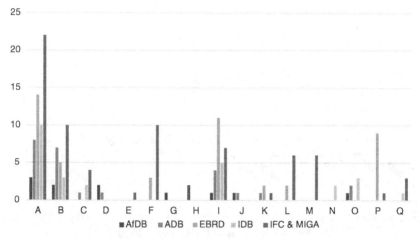

Figure 4.4 Findings of non-compliance from claims submitted to the compliance investigation function of the IAMs of the MDBs, 1994–2019.

most-frequent policy breach for the European Bank for Reconstruction and Development and Inter-American Development Bank is for Disclosure of Information, which indicates that the Banks are not upholding this procedural environmental right. This is also seriously breached by the World Bank Group although not as much as Natural Habitats; and the Asian Development Bank but not as much as its Involuntary Resettlement policy (or resettling people with their agreement). In comparison, the numbers are smaller for the African Development Bank, but it has breached Involuntary Resettlement, Gender and Development, and Poverty Reduction more than its Disclosure of Information policy. For the World Bank, five other policies were breached more than its Disclosure of Information,[48] which was found not to be compliant in eight of the thirty-seven cases of non-compliance (see Figure 4.5). Although there is a variation of policy breaches, the IAMs do provide recourse for grievances pertaining to procedural environmental rights.

With regards to the rights of nature, the key policy breached by the Banks is environmental and social impact assessment, which speaks to the challenge of the Banks in adequately assessing the needs of nature in relation to the project. However, as noted at the outset of Section 3, the claims coming to the Banks' IAMs do constitute less than 1 per cent of the Banks' annual project portfolios, highlighting that while this may not capture all of the problems associated with international development financing, that the Banks might be conducting and

---

[48] Owing to the more detailed, specific environmental and social protection standards by the World Bank, these are represented separately (as detailed in Section 2).

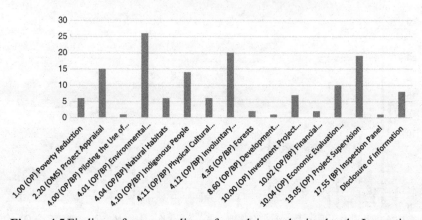

Figure 4.5 Findings of non-compliance from claims submitted to the Inspection Panel of the World Bank, 1994–2019

adequately adhering to environmental assessments most of the time. The environmental assessment recognises the right of nature to exist, as it seeks to mitigate the impact of development on it. The environmental assessment does consider the right of nature to regenerate where economically feasible and, as noted earlier, the project site may exclude necessary components of ecosystems that operate as a whole (the right of nature to regenerate when damaged). The Banks do sometimes incorporate larger regional environmental assessments to address ecosystem effects but the IAMs can only address the project site financed by that specific Bank and as it pertains to the people that submit the claim. It is unclear therefore whether the right to be restored when damaged is considered through this process.

Conclusion

Section 4 has identified how the IAMs seek to provide access to justice in environmental matters through the provision of compliance investigations into whether harm has resulted from the actions or inactions of the multilateral development banks. It documented how the IAM compliance investigation function operates, and how claims move through the stages from appraisal, to a recommendation for investigation, to undertaking an investigation and producing findings and recommendations. The IAMs now also have monitoring functions, and some have advisory powers that align with the UN Guiding Principles that IGMs should be a source of continuous learning. The section highlighted that claimants often seek recourse for a lack of access to information, a lack of participation and consent, and the rights of nature independent of claimants' dependence on the environment. This demonstrates that the IAMs are being used not just for recourse for breaches of procedural environmental rights but also the rights of nature. The section then demonstrated that the IAMs do find that the Banks are non-compliant with their environmental and social protection standards in their investigations, showing a willingness of the IAMs to reveal environmental and social harm caused by the Banks. The IAMs have increasingly been given power to monitor the Banks to bring them back into compliance. However, research is needed to determine whether this contributes to the point of providing remedy for the harm. While the IAMs can therefore provide recourse for environmental and social harm, there remains a larger question as to whether recourse for people through the IAMs protects the rights of nature in accordance with states' commitments to multilateral environmental agreements (Zalcberg 2012).

5 Providing Effective International Recourse for Environmental and Social Harm

This Element began with the question as to whether environmental and social harm could be effectively addressed at the international level. Owing to the different aims of states seeking legal recourse, this Element focused on the ability of communities to access non-legal international grievance mechanisms for justice in environmental matters. This is important given the proliferation of IGMs globally as a means of resolving grievances emerging from the interventions of transnational and international actors in developing countries. As highlighted in Section 1, while environmental and social harm caused by actors operating beyond the state is not new, over time the volume of interactions has increased, resulting in further environmental degradation with the likelihood for conflict and greater harm, and international actors are increasingly working together in ways that blur the ability of people adversely affected to hold them responsible and accountable. IGMs seek to provide direct recourse for people and their environments adversely affected by the actions of transnational and international actors. The IGMs vary substantially from the MDBs' independent accountability mechanisms, to Ombudsman for international organisations, to multi-stakeholder forums, and international framework agreements. The Element specifically examines the independent accountability mechanisms of the MDBs, which can provide recourse for people to air their grievance if the social and environmental harm has been caused by the acts or omission of the multilateral development banks.

Here we recount the main arguments of the Element and suggest a future research agenda. In Section 1, the Element highlighted the emergence of the rights of people to their environment in procedural terms. This included the right to information and participation regarding issues affecting their environment as well as having access to recourse and remedy. These are enshrined in the 1998 Convention to on Access to Information, Public Participation in Decision-Making and Access to Justice in Environmental Matters (the Aarhus Convention), and the 2018 Escazú Agreement, as well as specific multilateral environmental agreements, and are increasingly referenced in the UN and in World Bank protection standards, although the latter does not see them as 'rights'. The Element also questioned whether the rights of nature (to exist, to regenerate, and to be restored when damaged) were able to be addressed given the focus of the IGMs to providing recourse to people. This is vital as environment cannot speak for itself and environmental change is accelerating on a global scale.

Section 2 then analysed IGMs in relation to two distinct but increasingly overlapping international standards: the UN Guiding Principles for Business and Human Rights in relation to human rights and transnational corporations and other business enterprises, and the World Bank protection standards that have been emulated by other public and private funders. The section outlined the evolution of the Guiding Principles and the World Bank's standards and how they include procedural environmental rights even if they do not explicitly frame them as such. There are detailed criteria for how IGMs should operate, which emerged in parallel from the UN and the IAMs of the MDBs: legitimate, accessible, predictable, equitable, transparent, rights-compatible, and a source of continuous learning for the Guiding Principles, and be accessible, transparent, independent, impartial, act with integrity and be professional, and be responsive for the IAMs (Lewis 2012). However, there is little information on how MNCs and business enterprises are meeting criteria for their IGMs to provide effective access to justice in environmental matters. This Element provides evidence of the activities of the IAMs in upholding people's procedural rights, and the rights of nature, including as well as beyond, the needs of people. The data from the content analysis of original claims reveals that 49 per cent of all original claims identified a lack of access to information, 54 per cent of claims were aggrieved by a lack of access to participation, while 27 per cent of claims referenced harm to nature outside of the direct impact this would have on claimants.

This Element therefore probed if and how the IAMs provide recourse. Apart from the World Bank's Inspection Panel, the IAMs have 'problem-solving' components not dissimilar to broader Ombuds processes, as well as compliance investigations that seek to identify the link between harm and the actions or omissions of the MDBs. Section 3 identified how people are engaged in problem-solving, seeking recourse for grievances including a lack of access to information and participation but also concern for the environment outside their own needs. While only a quarter of the claims went to the problem-solving initiative with these grievances, they were more likely to go to mediation based on harm to nature (48 per cent). However, the results of the analysis of the problem-solving process indicates that there is a high rate of unsuccessful outcomes from communities attempting to engage directly with the Banks and project sponsors. This is because the process is dependent on the willingness of the parties to engage in coming to agreement as to how to address the grievance. While there are individual variations in some Banks that may indicate unjust practices, overall, the IAM process does seem to provide access to justice in environmental matters through problem-solving. The biggest reason for the process to fail is the unwillingness of the parties to engage with one another to address the problem. This speaks to the voluntary nature of the process. While IGMs overall are predicated on voluntarism, this should not be the only means of seeking recourse given that there may be no access to remedy.

Section 4 therefore investigated the way in which compliance investigations operate. The data of the original claims demonstrates that claimants were more likely to go to a compliance investigation to show that the lack of enforcing procedural rights led to harm caused by the Banks. Again, while there is some variation among the Banks, revealing some Bank-specific unjust practices, the compliance investigation process does seem robust in investigating Bank compliance with its own protection standards. The section documented how the IAMs investigate whether harm has resulted from the actions or inactions of the MDBs. Claims move through the stages: from appraisal, to a recommendation for investigation, to undertaking an investigation, producing findings and recommendations, and monitoring to bring the projects into policy compliance. Moreover, some of the IAMs have advisory powers that align with the Guiding Principles that IGMs should be a source of continuous learning. The IAMs do find Bank non-compliance with their environmental and social protection standards in their investigations, but even with monitoring to enforce compliance it is unclear whether this contributes to providing remedy for the harm. Ultimately this means that more local-level research is required to identify the benefits of using these mechanisms for communities being harmed by transnational and international processes like development projects.

The volume therefore achieved its three aims: first, it identified the underlying normative standards underpinning IGMs including their conceptions of human rights and environmental and social standards; second, it outlined the processes for providing access to justice in environmental matters through an investigation of the IAMs; and third, it identified whether the problem-solving processes for grievance redressal work better than compliance investigations for providing recourse. Further research on the specific practices of each Bank's

IAM, and the practices of IGMs more generally will be able to answer whether the trend towards international non-judicial grievance mechanisms is helpful for upholding procedural environmental rights, the rights of nature, and whether these meet states' adherence to multilateral environmental agreements. While limited, the IAMs can provide access to recourse but more needs to be done as to whether this can translate into a fair and effective remedy for communities.

Contribution and Future Research Agenda

What do the IGMs tell us about global environmental governance? Recognisably, the shift from the national to the international is not just occurring in terms of political economy, but also attempts to govern transnational and international actors for their negative environmental impacts. The shift upwards has also led to an increase in efforts to provide accountability, including recourse and remedy. While most IGMs focus on recourse, there is not enough known about the processes to identify whether remedies are proffered and succeed in addressing grievances. As noted by Lukas et al. (2016), IGMs are weaker than judicial mechanisms in enforcing behaviour. The research here can point to improvements for some communities after making claims to the IAMs, but further research is needed as to how this compared with other options available to protect procedural environmental rights and the rights of nature.

Recognising the limitations of international grievance mechanisms in relation to communities and nature should not detract from the importance of the provision of international recourse. Over the last two decades, global governance has been criticised for its lack of transparency, accountability, legitimacy, and democratic processes. The ongoing drive towards ever more inter-linked global markets, reinforces the need for feedback mechanisms at the global level that can provide impetus to make global level changes to limit localised harm (where specific groups suffer for the benefit of others, while the environment continues to be devalued). Although there is a proliferation of global environmental governance, international grievance mechanisms need not be additional separate entities that add to fragmentation and duplication. There are arguments in favour of independent Ombuds for transnational and international actors, but there is much room to improve on what we have already.

Three issues remain. First, there is not enough research on how the environment is being protected through IGMs in terms of harmed ecosystems' right to exist, be repaired, and allowed to regenerate. IGMs that follow the UN Guiding Principles are more geared towards human rights than the environment, while the World Bank–promulgated environmental and social standards shy away from human rights but have robust environmental provisions that need to be enforced. Second, we do not know the extent to which the environment continues to be devastated by transnational and international actors that choose to forego financing from the MDBs considering claims to the IAMs. In other words, until there are robust provisions for recourse and remedy for all transnational and international actors, there remain loopholes through which harm may continue. The IAMs can only provide recourse for communities if they are linked to projects that are financed by the MDBs. And corporate actors will choose to repay or decline a loan to avoid being held to account for their actions. Given the lack of transparency for corporate actors, IAMs remain just one means for addressing harm within specific constraints. Even with the proliferation of IGMs, the perennial question remains: Who holds the IGMs to account? Finally, while this analysis goes some way towards understanding how recourse can be provided, are the IAMs the best means for protecting the rights of nature? Communities are using the independent accountability mechanisms to signal harm to ecosystems, but these remain very much within the framework for procedural environmental rights. Indeed, the IAMs limit their investigations to harm at the project site, rather than the health of an ecosystem. Given the increasing recognition of inter-linkages within and between Earth systems, we need to be conscious of whether attempts to address environmental harm should be examined through an ecocentric rather than anthropocentric lens, and whether we have the time to do it.

Abbreviations

AfDB	African Development Bank
ADB	Asian Development Bank – ADB
CAO	Compliance Advisor/Ombudsman for the World Bank Group
EBRD	European Bank for Reconstruction and Development – EBRD
IAMs	Independent Accountability Mechanisms of the multilateral development banks
IDB	Inter-American Development Bank
IFC	International Finance Corporation, an arm of the World Bank Group
IGMs	International grievance mechanisms
MDBs	Multilateral development banks
MEAs	Multilateral environmental agreements
MNCs	Multinational corporations
MICI	Independent Consultation and Investigation Mechanism of the InterAmerican Development Bank (known by its Spanish acronym MICI)
MIGA	Multilateral Investment Guarantee Agency, an arm of the World Bank Group
NGOs	Nongovernment organisations
OECD	Organisation for Economic Cooperation and Development
UN	United Nations
UNDRIP	United Nations Declaration on the Rights of Indigenous Peoples

Bibliography

Abouharb, M., and D. Cingranelli, 2007, *Human Rights and Structural Adjustment*, Cambridge: Cambridge University Press.

Alter, K., 2014, *The New Terrain of International Law*, Princeton: Princeton University Press.

Andonova, L., 2017, *Governance Entrepreneurs: International Organizations and the Rise of Public–Private Partnerships*, Cambridge: Cambridge University Press.

Balaton Chrimes, S. and F. Haines, 2015, "The Depoliticisation of Accountability Processes for Land Based Grievances, and the IFC CAO," *Global Policy* 6 (4): 446–454.

Bell, C., 2009, 'Transitional Justice, Interdisciplinarity and the State of the 'Field' or 'Non-Field', *The International Journal of Transitional Justice*, 3: 5–27.

Biermann, F., 2014, *Earth System Governance: World Politics in the Anthropocene*, Cambridge: MIT Press.

Biermann, F., and B. Siebenhuner, 2009, *Managers of Global Change: The Influence of International Environmental Bureaucracies*, Cambridge: MIT Press.

Bilchitz, D., and S. Deva (eds.), 2013, *Human Rights Obligations of Business: Beyond the Corporate Responsibility to Respect?* Cambridge: Cambridge University Press.

Block-Lieb, S., and T. Halliday, 2017, *Global Lawmakers: International Organizations in the Crafting of World Markets*, Cambridge: Cambridge University Press.

Butt, N., F. Lambrick, M. Menton, and A. Renwick, 2019, 'The Supply Chain of Violence', *Nature Sustainability* 2: 742–7.

Carl, S., 2018, 'The History and Evolution of the Ombudsman Model', in *Research Handbook on the Ombudsman*, edited by Marc Hertogh and Richard Kirkham, Cheltenham: Edward Elgar: 17–33.

Carmen, J., and J. Agyeman (eds.), 2011, *Environmental Inequalities Beyond Borders: Local Perspectives on Global Injustices*, Cambridge: MIT Press.

CIEL, 2016, 'NGO Response: Proposed World Bank Safeguards Represent Dangerous Set-Back to Key Environmental and Social Protections, Press Release 22 July.www.ciel.org/news/safeguard-policy-endangers-rights/. Accessed 19 December 2016.

Clapham, A., 2006, *Human Rights Obligations of Non-State Actors*, Oxford: Oxford University Press.

Clark, D., Fox, J., and K. Treakle, 2003, *Demanding Accountability: Civil-Society Claims and the World Bank Inspection Panel*, Lanham: Rowman and Littlefield.

Compliance Advisor Ombudsman (CAO), 2019, *2018 Annual Report*, Washington, DC, World Bank Group. www.cao-ar18.org/grievance-mechanism-article/index.html. Accessed 18 October 2019.

Compliance Advisor/Ombudsman (CAO), 2006, *Annual Report: 2005–2006*, Washington, DC, IFC and MIGA, CAO.

Conca, K., 2015, *An Unfinished Foundation: The United Nations and Global Environmental Governance*, Oxford: Oxford University Press.

Cutler, C., 2003, *Private Power and Global Authority: Transnational Merchant Law in the Global Economy*, Cambridge: Cambridge University Press.

Darrow, M., 2003, *Between Light and Shadow: The World Bank, the International Monetary Fund and International Human Rights Law*, Oxford and Portland, OR: Hart Publishing.

Earth System Governance, 2018, Science and Implementation Plan of the Earth System Governance Project, www.earthsystemgovernance.org/wp-content/uploads/2018/11/Earth-System-Governance-Science-Plan-2018.pdf. Accessed 9 August 2019.

European Bank for Reconstruction and Development, 2012, *Compliance Review Report: Complaint: Tbilisi Railway Bypass, Request Number 2011/01, 2011/02, 2011/03*, London, EBRD. www.ebrd.com/work-with-us/project-finance/project-complaint-mechanism/pcm-register.html. Accessed 5 May 2020.

Foster, C., 2011, *Science and the Precautionary Principle in International Courts and Tribunals*, Cambridge: Cambridge University Press.

Fox, J., and D. L. Brown (eds.), 1998, *The Struggle for Accountability: The World Bank, NGOs and Grassroots Movements*, Cambridge, MA: MIT Press.

Fujita, S., 2013, *The World Bank, Asian Development Bank and Human Rights*, Cheltenham: Edward Elgar.

Harrison, T., 2004, 'What Is Success in Ombuds Processes? Evaluation of a University Ombudsman', *Conflict Resolution Quarterly* 21 (3): 313–35.

Hertogh, M., and R. Kirkham, 2018, 'The Ombudsman and Administrative Justice: From Promise to Performance', in *Research Handbook on the Ombudsman*, edited by Marc Hertogh and Richard Kirkham, Cheltenham: Edward Elgar: 1–15.

Hoffman, F., and F. Megret, 2005, 'Fostering Human Rights Accountability: An Ombudsman for the United Nations', *Global Governance* 11: 43–63.

Hofmann, H., 2017, 'The Developing Role of the European Ombudsman', in *Accountability in the EU: The Role of the European Ombudsman*, edited by Herwig Hofmann and Jacques Ziller, Cheltenham: Edward Elgar: 1–27.

Huijstee, M., K. Genovese, C. Daniel, and S. Singh, 2016, *Glass Half Full: The State of Accountability in Development Finance*. Report by 11 NGOs. www .somo.nl/glass-half-full-2/. Accessed 19 December 2016.

Hunter, D., 2008, 'Civil Society Networks and the Development of Environmental Standards at International Financial Institutions', *Chicago Journal of International Law* 8 (2): 437–77.

Hunter, D., 2003, 'Using the World Bank Inspection Panel to Defend the Interests of Project-Affected People', *Chicago Journal of International Law* 4 (1): Article 14.

Independent Consultation and Investigation Mechanism (ICIM), 2011, Annual Report 2010, IDB. www.iadb.org/en/mici/publications,1768.html. Accessed 9 April 2014.

Independent Consultation and Investigation Mechanism (ICIM), 2011b, CR-MICI001-2011, Closing Report of the Consultation Phase Loans, 2421/BL-NI, 1908/OC-CR and 2016/BL-HO 'Proposal for an Additional Financing of Cost Overruns for the Central American Electric Interconnection System (SIEPAC) Project and Reallocation of Resources from Loans'. Washington, DC, IDB. www.iadb.org/en/mici/chronological-public-registry%2C19181 .html. Accessed 11 May 2020.

Independent Review Mechanism, 2011, *Annual Report for 2011*, Tunis, AfDB.

Independent Review Mechanism, 2010, *Notice of Registration: Request for Compliance Review and/or Problem-solving Request No.: RQ2010/01, Country: Morocco Project: Construction of the Marrakech – Agadir Motorway*, African Development Bank. www.afdb.org/en/independent-review-mechanism/management-of-complaints/registered-requests/rq-20101-morocco. Accessed 9 May 2020.

Independent Review Mechanism, 2007, *Notice of Registration: Request for Compliance Review, Request No.: RQ 2007/01), Country: Uganda, Bujagali Hydropower Project and Bujagali Interconnection Project*, African Development Bank. www.afdb.org/en/independent-review-mech anism/management-of-complaints/registered-requests/rq-20071-uganda. Accessed 9 May 2020.

Inspection Panel, 2009, *Accountability at the World Bank: The Inspection Panel at 15 Years*, Washington, DC: The Inspection Panel, World Bank.

International Finance Corporation, 2012, IFC Sustainability Framework: Policy and Performance Standards on Environmental and Social Sustainability, Access to Information Policy, Washington, DC: World Bank Group. www.ifc.org/wps/wcm/connect/topics_ext_content/ifc_exter

nal_corporate_site/sustainability-at-ifc/policies-standards/ifcsustainability framework_2012. Accessed 18 October 2019.

International Finance Corporation, 2012b, *The International Bill of Human Rights and IFC Sustainability Framework*, Washington, DC: World Bank Group. www.ifc.org/wps/wcm/connect/topics_ext_content/ifc_external_cor porate_site/sustainability-at-ifc/publications/ibhr_ifc_sustainability_frame work. Accessed 18 October 2019.

International Ombudsman Institute, 2012, Bylaws, Adopted by the General Assembly in Wellington, New Zealand, 13 November 2012.

Kaufman, J., and K. McDonnell, 2015, 'Community-Driven Operational Grievance Mechanisms', *Business and Human Rights Journal* 1: 127–32.

Kauffman, C., and L. Sheehan, 2019, 'The Rights of Nature: Guiding Our Responsibilities through Standards', in *Environmental Rights: The Development of Standards*, edited by Stephen Turner, Cambridge: Cambridge University Press: 342–66.

Keck, M., and Sikkink, K., 1998, *Activists Beyond Borders: Advocacy Networks in International Politics*, Ithaca and London: Cornell University Press.

Keonig-Archibugi, M., and K. Macdonald, 2017, 'The Role of Beneficiaries in Transnational Regulatory Processes', *American Academy of Political and Social Science Annals* 670: 36–67.

Keonig-Archibugi, M., and K. Macdonald, 2013, 'Accountability-by-Proxy in Transnational Non-State Governance', *Governance: An International Journal of Policy and Administration* 26 (3): 499–522.

Kingsbury, B., Krisch, N., and R. Stewart, 2005 'Emergence of Global Administrative Law', *Law and Contemporary Problems* 68 (15): 15–62.

Lewis, K., 2012, Citizen Driven Accountability for Sustainable Development, Report Prepared for the Rio+20 Conference by the Independent Accountability Mechanism Network. www.opic.gov/sites/default/files/files/ citizen-driven-accountibility.pdf. Accessed June 2018.

Lukas, K., B. Linder, A. Kutrzeba, and C. Sprenger, 2016, *Corporate Accountability: The Role and Impact of Non-judicial Grievance*, Cheltenham: Edward Elgar.

Mares, R., 2019, 'Securing Human Rights through Risk-Management Methods: Breakthrough or Misalignment?' *Leiden Journal of International Law* 32: 517–35.

Mason, M., 2005, *The New Accountability: Environmental Responsibility Across Borders*, London: Earthscan.

Matejova, M., S. Parker, and P. Dauvergne, 2018, 'The Politics of Repressing Environmentalists as Agents of Foreign Influence', *Australian Journal of International Affairs* 72 (2): 145–62.

Mattli, W., and T. Diez, 2014, *International Arbitration and Global Governance*, Oxford: Oxford University Press.

McIntyre, O., and S. Nanwani, 2019, *The Practice of Independent Accountability Mechanisms (IAMs): Towards Good Governance in Development Finance*, Leiden, Brill.

Macdonald, K., and T. Macdonald, 2017, 'Liquid Authority and Political Legitimacy in Transnational Governance', *International Theory* 9 (2): 329–51.

Macdonald, K., and M. Miller-Dawkins, 2015, "Accountability in Public International Development Finance," Global Policy 6: 429–434.

Mitchell, R. 2002–2019. *International Environmental Agreements Database Project* (Version 2018.1), http://iea.uoregon.edu/. Accessed 16 July 2019.

Moravcsik, A., 2004, 'Is there a "Democratic Deficit" in World Politics?: A Framework for Analysis', *Government and Opposition* 39 (2): 336–63.

Naudé-Fourie, A., 2016, *World Bank Accountability – In Theory and in Practice*, The Hague: Eleven International Publishing.

Ognibene, L., and A. Kariuki, 2019, 'Standards in the Procedural Rights of Multilateral Environmental Agreements', in *Environmental Rights: The Development of Standards*, edited by S. Turner, D. Shelton, J. Razzaque, O. McIntyre, and J. May, Cambridge, Cambridge University Press: 174–94.

Organisation for Economic Cooperation and Development, 2018, *Multilateral Development Finance: Towards a New Pact on Multilateralism to Achieve the 2030 Agenda Together*, Geneva, OECD. www.oecd.org/dac/financing-sustainable-development/development-finance-topics/Multilateral-Development-Finance-Highlights-2018.pdf. Accessed 20 September 2019.

OECD 2017, *OECD Due Diligence Guidance for Meaningful Stakeholder Engagement in the Extractive Sector*, Paris: OECD Publishing.

OECD, 2011, *OECD Guidelines for Multinational Enterprises*, Paris: OECD Publishing.

Pahuja, S., 2011, *Decolonising International Law: Development, Economic Growth and the Politics of Universality*, Cambridge: Cambridge University Press.

Park, S., unpublished manuscript, *The Good Hegemon: US Power, Accountability as Justice, and the Multilateral Development Banks*.

Park, S., 2019, *Claims Submitted to the Multilateral Development Bank Accountability Mechanisms: 1994–2016*. Sydney: The University of Sydney. http://dx.doi.org/10.25910/5bdb90e22bf46

Park, S., 2017, 'Accountability as Justice for the Multilateral Development Banks? Borrower Opposition and Bank Avoidance to US Power and Influence', *Review of International Political Economy*, 24 (5): 776–801.

Park, S., 2013, 'Transnational Environmental Activism', in *The Handbook of Global Climate and Environment Policy*, edited by Robert Falkner, Chichester UK: John Wiley & Sons: 268–85.

Park, S., 2010, *World Bank Group interactions with Environmentalists: Changing International Organisation Identities*. Manchester, UK: Manchester University Press.

Park, S., and T. Kramarz, eds. 2019, *Global Environmental Governance and the Accountability Trap*. Cambridge: MIT Press.

Passoni, C., A. Rosenbaum, and E. Vermunt, 2016, *Empowering the Inspection Panel: The Impact of the World Bank's Safeguards Review*. Report, New York University School of Law. www.iilj.org/publications/empowering-the-inspection-panel/. Accessed 19 December 2016.

Partzsch, L., 2020, *Alternatives to Multilateralism: New Forms of Social and Environmental Governance*, Cambridge, MIT Press.

Peel, J., 2011, *Science and Risk Regulation in International Law*, Cambridge, Cambridge University Press.

Razzaque, J., 2019, 'A Stock-Taking of FPIC Standards in International Environmental Law', in *Environmental Rights: The Development of Standards*, edited by S. Turner, D. Shelton, J. Razzaque, O. McIntyre, and J. May, Cambridge: Cambridge University Press: 195–221.

Richard, V., 2017, 'Accountability by Proxy? The Ripple Effects of MDBs' International Accountability Mechanisms on the Private Sector', in *Conceptualizing Accountability in International Financial Law*, edited by P. Vargiu, F. Seatzu, and F. Esu. halshs-01298135. Accessed 12 August 2019.

Richard, V., no date, 'More Details on the Project', *IGMs Project*. www.igms-project.org/. Accessed 13 August 2019.

Rodrigues, M.G., 2003, *Global Environmentalism and Local Politics: Transnational Advocacy Networks in Brazil, Ecuador, and India*, New York, SUNY Press.

Ruggie, J., 2013, *Just Business: Multinational Corporations and Human Rights*, New York: W.W Norton and Company.

Ruggie, J., 2001, 'Global-governance.net: The Global Compact as Learning Network', *Global Governance* 7: 371–8.

Ruggie, J. and T. Nelson, 2015, "Human Rights and the OECD Guidelines for Multinational Enterprises: Normative Innovations and Implementation Challenges," Faculty Research Working Paper Series, Harvard Kennedy School, RWP15-045.

Sagafi-Nejad, T., and J. Dunning, 2008, *The UN and Transnational Corporations: From Code of Conduct to Global Compact*, Bloomington, Indianapolis: Indiana University Press.

Sarfaty, G., 2009, "Why Culture Matters in International Institutions: The Marginality of Human Rights at the World Bank," *American Journal of International Law*, 103: 647–683.

Schmitt, P., 2017, *Access to Justice and International Organizations: The Case of Individual Victims of Human Rights Violations*, Cheltenham UK, Edward Elgar.

Schrijver, N., 2010, *Development without Destruction: The UN and Global Resource Management*, Bloomington: Indiana University Press.

Sovacool, B. 2017, 'Monitoring the Moneylenders: Institutional Accountability and Environmental Governance at the World Bank's Inspection Panel', *The Extractives Industry and Society* 4: 893–903.

Special Representative of the Secretary-General on the Issue of Human Rights and Transnational Corporations and other Business Enterprises, 2011, *Guiding Principle on Business and Human Rights: Implementing the United Nations 'Protect, Respect and Remedy' Framework*, Geneva, United Nations, U.N. Doc. A/HRC/17/31.

Steffen, W., K. Richardson, J. Rockström et al. 2015. 'Planetary Boundaries: Guiding Human Development on a Changing Planet', *Science* 347 (6223): 1259855.

Tallberg, J., T. Sommerer, T. Squatrito, and C. Jönsson, 2013, *The Opening up of International Organizations: Transnational Access in Global Governance*, New York: Cambridge University Press.

Temper, L., F. Demaria, A. Scheidel, D. Del Bene, and J. Martinez-Alier, 2018, 'The Global Environmental Justice Atlas (EJAtlas): Ecological Distribution Conflicts as Forces for Sustainability', *Sustainability Science* 13 (3): 573–84.

Thompson, B., 2017, 'Determining Criteria to Evaluate Outcomes of Businesses' Provision of Remedy: Applying a Human Rights-Based Approach', *Business and Human Rights Journal*, 2: 55–85.

Tienhaara, K., 2009, *The Expropriation of Environmental Governance*, Cambridge: Cambridge University Press.

Turner, S., D. Shelton, J. Razzaque, O. McIntyre, J. May (eds.), 2019, *Environmental Rights: The Development of Standards*, Cambridge: Cambridge University Press.

United Nations, 2018, *Report of the Special Rapporteur on the Issue of Human Rights Obligations relating to the Enjoyment of a Safe, Clean, Healthy and Sustainable Environment*, Human Rights Council 37th Session, A/HRC/37/59. https://undocs.org/A/HRC/37/59. Accessed 14 October 2019.

United Nations, 2015, *Report of the Special Rapporteur on Extreme Poverty and Human Rights*, United Nations General Assembly 70th Session, A/70/274. www.un.org/en/ga/search/view_doc.asp?symbol=A/70/274. Accessed 14 October 2019.

United Nations, 2011, *Guiding Principles on Business and Human Rights: Implementing the United Nations 'Protect, Respect and Remedy' Framework*, New York and Geneva, United Nations. www.ohchr.org/Documents/Publications/GuidingPrinciplesBusinessHR_EN.pdf. Accessed 8 July 2016.

United Nations Commission on Human Rights, 2003, 'Norms on the responsibilities of transnational corporations and other business enterprises with regard to human rights' Sub-Commission on the Promotion and Protection of Human Rights, Fifty-fifth session, Agenda item 4, Resolution 16/2003, E/CN.4/Sub.2/2003/12/Rev.2

United Nations Environment Programme, 2010, *Putting Rio Principle 10 Into Action: An Implementation Guide for the UNEP Bali Guidelines for the Development of National Legislation on Access to Information, Public Participation and Access to Justice in Environmental Matters*, Geneva, UNEP. www.unenvironment.org/ru/node/10214. Accessed 24 September 2019.

United Nations Global Compact, 2019, 'The Ten Principles of the UN Global Compact', United Nations. www.unglobalcompact.org/what-is-gc/mission/principles. Accessed 6 October 2019.

Weissbrodt, D. and M. Kruger, 2003, 'Norms on the Responsibilities of Transnational Corporations and Other Business Enterprises', *American Journal of International Law* 97 (4): 901–22.

Wellens, K., 2002, *Remedies against International Organisations*, Cambridge: Cambridge University Press.

World Bank, 2019, Inspection Panel. www.inspectionpanel.org/. Accessed 14 August 2019.

World Bank, 2019b, *Annual Report*, Washington, DC. World Bank. www.worldbank.org/en/about/annual-report. Accessed 17 September 2019.

World Bank, 2016, 'The New Environmental and Social Framework', Safeguards, World Bank website. web.worldbank.org/WBSITE/EXTERNAL/PROJECTS/EXTPOLICIES/EXTSAFEPOL/0,menuPK:584441~pagePK:64168427~piPK:64168435~theSitePK:584435,00.html. Accessed 16 December 2016.

Wright, C., 2007, 'From 'Safeguards' to 'Sustainability': the Evolution of Environmental Discourse inside the International Finance Corporation', in

The World Bank and Governance: A Decade of Reform and Reaction, edited by Diane Stone and Christopher Wright, New York: Routledge: 67–87.

Zagelmeyer, S., L. Bianchi, and A. Shemberg, 2018, 'Non-State Based Non-Judicial Grievance Mechanisms (NSBGM): An Exploratory Analysis', A report prepared for the Office of the UN High Commissioner for Human Rights, University of Manchester. www.ohchr.org/Documents/Issues/Business/ARP/ManchesterStudy.pdf. Accessed 14 August 2019.

Zalcberg, J., 2012, 'The World Bank Inspection Panel: A Tool for Ensuring the World Bank's Compliance with International Law', *Macquarie Journal of International and Comparative Environmental Law* 8 (2): 1–19.

Zappile, T., 2016, 'Sub-Regional Development Banks: Development as Usual?' in *Global Economic Governance and the Development Practices of the Multilateral Development Banks*, edited by Susan Park and Jonathan R. Strand, Abingdon: Routledge.

Ziai, A., 2016, "Can the subaltern file claims? The World Bank Inspection Panel and subaltern articulation," *Momentum Quarterly* 5 (4): 255–264.

Acknowledgements

I would like to acknowledge the fantastic work my research assistants have done in collecting material for me: Roland Harris, Eda Gunaydin, and Madison Cartwright. Always professional and hardworking, it is a real pleasure to have worked with these great people while they continue their own journeys.

To Matt and my boys, always.

About the Author

Susan Park is Professor of Global Governance in the Department of Government and International Relations at the University of Sydney. She focuses on how state and non-state actors seek to influence International Organisations like the Multilateral Development Banks (MDBs) and global governance more broadly to become greener and more accountable. She is an Associate Editor of the journal *Global Environmental Politics* and is Co-Convenor with Dr Kramarz (University of Toronto) of the Earth Systems Governance (ESG) Task Force 'Accountability in Global Environmental Governance'. She is currently a Senior Hans Fischer Fellow at the Technical University of Munich (2019-2022).

Cambridge Elements$^{\equiv}$

Elements of Earth System Governance

Frank Biermann
Utrecht University

Frank Biermann is Research Professor of Global Sustainability Governance with the Copernicus Institute of Sustainable Development, Utrecht University, the Netherlands. He is the founding Chair of the Earth System Governance Project, a global transdisciplinary research network launched in 2009; and Editor-in-Chief of the new peer-reviewed journal *Earth System Governance* (Elsevier). In April 2018, he won a European Research Council Advanced Grant for a research program on the steering effects of the Sustainable Development Goals.

Aarti Gupta
Wageningen University

Aarti Gupta is Professor of Global Environmental Governance at the Environmental Policy Group of Wageningen University, the Netherlands. She has been a Lead Faculty in the Earth System Governance Project since 2014 and served as one of five Coordinating Lead Authors of the recently issued New Directions ESG Science and Implementation Plan. As of November 2018, she is a member of the ESG Project's Scientific Steering Committee. She is also Associate Editor of the journal *Global Environmental Politics*.

About the series

Linked with the Earth System Governance Project, this exciting new series will provide concise but authoritative studies of the governance of complex socio-ecological systems, written by world-leading scholars. Highly interdisciplinary in scope, the series will address governance processes and institutions at all levels of decision-making, from local to global, within a planetary perspective that seeks to align current institutions and governance systems with the fundamental 21st Century challenges of global environmental change and earth system transformations.

Elements in this series will present cutting edge scientific research, while also seeking to contribute innovative transformative ideas towards better governance. A key aim of the series is to present policy-relevant research that is of interest to both academics and policy-makers working on earth system governance.

More information about the Earth System Governance project can be found at: www.earthsystemgovernance.org

Cambridge Elements ☰

Elements of Earth System Governance

Elements in the series

Deliberative Global Governance
John S. Dryzek et al.

Environmental Rights in Earth System Governance: Democracy Beyond Democracy
Walter F. Baber and Robert V. Bartlett

The Making of Responsible Innovation
Phil Macnaghten

Environmental Recourse at the Multilateral Development Banks
Susan Park

A full series listing is available at www.cambridge.org/EESG

Printed in the United States
By Bookmasters